585 Raids and Counting

585 Raids and Counting

*Memoir of an American Soldier
in the Solomon Islands, 1942–1945*

ALEX KUNEVICIUS

McFarland & Company, Inc., Publishers
Jefferson, North Carolina, and London

LIBRARY OF CONGRESS CATALOGUING-IN-PUBLICATION DATA

Kunevicius, Alex, 1919–
    585 raids and counting : memoir of an American soldier in the Solomon Islands, 1942–1945 / Alex Kunevicius.
       p.   cm.
    Includes index.

    ISBN 978-0-7864-6446-3
    softcover : 50# alkaline paper ∞

    1. Kunevicius, Alex, 1919– 2. World War, 1939–1945 — Solomon Islands. 3. World War, 1939–1945 — Personal narratives, American. 4. United States. Army. Ordnance Company, 22nd. 5. United States. Army — Ordnance and ordnance stores — History — 20th century. 6. United States. Army — Military life — History — 20th century. 7. Soldiers — United States — Biography. 8. Soldiers — Solomon Islands — Biography. 9. Solomon Islands — History, Military — 20th century. I Title. II. Title: Five hundred eighty-five raids and counting.
D767.98.K86 2011
940.54'26593092 — dc22
[B]   2011015490

BRITISH LIBRARY CATALOGUING DATA ARE AVAILABLE

© 2011 Alex Kunevicius. All rights reserved

No part of this book may be reproduced or transmitted in any form or by any means, electronic or mechanical, including photocopying or recording, or by any information storage and retrieval system, without permission in writing from the publisher.

Front cover image: soldiers walking through a South Pacific island jungle (National Guard Image Gallery)

Manufactured in the United States of America

McFarland & Company, Inc., Publishers
  Box 611, Jefferson, North Carolina 28640
    www.mcfarlandpub.com

A special thank you to my granddaughter
Kelly Kunevicius Cook,
who spent many hours editing and typing
my handwritten manuscript.

Table of Contents

Preface — 1

1. A Letter from the President: Fort Knox, Kentucky — 3
2. December 7, 1941: Trip to the Sea — 9
3. Australia — 31
4. New Caledonia — 37
5. St. Joseph's Cathedral — 56
6. Company on the Move — 65
7. Guadalcanal — 74
8. Lieutenant Ben Rabin and Men Arrive — 96
9. Christmas Day — 109
10. A Hand Grenade That Flies — 130
11. Company Split Up — 139
12. Sasavele Island First, Then New Georgia — 150
13. Kolambangara — 158
14. New Caledonia Again — 166
15. I See Land — 176

Index — 195

Preface

After completing army basic training in Fort Knox, Kentucky, standing in formation, we watched General George Patton drive by in his command car reviewing the newly trained troops. It was a proud moment for all of us. We were sure most of us would be placed in the general's armored division, a proud place to be.

It did not happen to me. A placement officer told me I was going to go into an ordnance company, a non-combat unit, and would be trained to fix guns. Where was the glory in that?

The newly formed 22nd Ordnance Company M.M. (Medium Maintenance) was small; about 120 drafted men, about a quarter of them from the Cleveland, Ohio, area. The collection of officers and sergeants commanding the unit were all professional soldiers. They were excellent teachers.

After army maneuvers in the state of Tennessee, the company traveled to Fort Leonard Wood, Missouri, our home for the next six months. In time, the men learned to fix guns, cannons, field instruments, anything not tied down, anything in sight.

The young men became friends and the company became a tight-knit family. The men worked hard, played some, and learned to eat and like army chow. Some weekends the men received leave to go to the nearby towns, visit the taverns and meet girls.

Come December 7, 1941. President Franklin D. Roosevelt proclaimed it a day of infamy. The Japanese attacked Pearl Harbor. Instantly the 22nd Ordnance Company was put on alert waiting for orders. Soon we traveled to the sea and went from the Brooklyn ship docks along the Atlantic coastline to the Panama Canal. Task Force 6814P, troop ships under General A. Patch's command, entered the vast blue Pacific.

In late February 1942 we landed in Melbourne, Australia, for a one

Preface

week stay. On March 12, 1942, about 17,000 army troops landed in the port city of Naumea, New Caledonia, to secure the island from a possible Japanese invasion.

The men of the 22nd Ordnance Company established a repair shop in the city of Naumea. We looked at, cleaned and repaired thousands of rifles, machine guns, and artillery pieces.

In New Caledonia, the famous Americal Division was born and under General Patch's command went on the first army offensive against the Japanese army in the Solomon Islands.

Guadalcanal, Talogi, Savo, Sasavele, New Georgia, Kolambangara and others: island invasion after invasion, hundreds of bombings, shellings, strafings and bombed out beaches was our way of life for the next two years. We kept the guns working and the cannons firing round after round and helped our fighting men secure island after island.

The 22nd Ordnance Company men spent four years together, sharing blood, sweat, and at times tears. Throughout the years our paths crossed many times and we kept our lifelong friendships.

My friends are gone now. One by one they strolled away into the unknown Island of Eternity, and if I really knew my buddies, I would bet they're waiting for me and asking the Great Redeemer to prepare a nice place for me.

God bless my buddies. God bless America.

**Americal Division
Under the Southern Cross**

1.

A Letter from the President: Fort Knox, Kentucky

It was a nice letter. The letter said, "Greetings." Because I was 21 years old, I was going to be drafted into the U.S. Army to serve our country for one year. I will never forget the date. It was March 5, 1941. I passed the physical examination with no problem, and I was subsequently sworn into the U.S. Army. That evening, at the railroad station, the newly-drafted men were saying their good-byes to their mothers and fathers, wives and girlfriends. Some of the wives and girlfriends were crying. I felt sorry for them and their guys too. I kissed my mother, father and sister, but I had no girlfriend to say good-bye to.

The next morning we arrived in Fort Knox, Kentucky. We were issued our uniforms. I received two shirts, some underwear, an old pair of cavalry britches with leggings, a large campaign hat, an old overcoat and a pair of shoes. The shoes were new. The tent I was assigned to had four bunks and a round belly coal stove. It was cold outside, and the latrine and shower stalls were about a hundred feet down the row of tents. We drilled all day and had lectures on military tactics and venereal diseases. We got to drive some old tanks and armored halftracks and even paraded in review for General George Patton.

After about six weeks of basic training, I was almost sure I would be placed in George Patton's First Armored Division, but it did not happen. During a screening interview a lieutenant asked me what my occupation was before I was drafted. I told him I worked for my father whose business was buying, repairing and selling rental properties. I told him I "can fix anything." Maybe it was my last remark that made the difference, because very soon after that I was assigned to a newly-formed 22nd Ordnance Company MM (Medium Maintenance), which was a weapons repair group.

The company comprised 120 men, about a quarter of them from Northern Ohio. Our commander was a regular army man, a tall Texan, Captain William Coyle. All of our sergeants were regular army enlisted men. Most of them were from the southern states and they were the cadre that put the company together.

Our first sergeant was Russell Van Meter, and the master sergeant was George Bridwell. We had a Sergeant Roy Horsley, Sergeant Charles Mooney, Sergeant Joseph White, Sergeant John Ankeny and more. They knew and loved army life and desperately tried to instill that feeling into us, their new recruits. Almost immediately after the company was formed, we participated in army maneuvers in the state of Tennessee. It turned out to be a very interesting four weeks. I think we were in the Blue Army and we were opposing the Green Army. On patrols we walked through bushes, corn fields and farmers' yards. Our food was edible; we slept in pup tents and took baths in cold creek water. We dealt with snakes, bugs, muskrats,

22nd Ordnance Company Artillery and Small Arms Repair Shop, Fort Leonard Wood, Missouri, 1941.

1. A Letter from the President

and some very friendly people, had some homemade moonshine and tasted some very bad drinking water.

One morning four of us men on patrol walking through the woods came to a farmhouse with a well. We were going to go to the well and get some water when we saw a lady come out of the house onto the porch. She was barefoot and she kicked something off the porch. It was a snake. She looked at us. One of the men asked her if we could get some water out of the well, if it was okay with her. We were thirsty.

The lady waved her hands in some sort of gesture and told us that the well was dry. There was no water, but she had something much better to drink if we cared to come in and visit with her. We looked at each other and went back into the woods and continued on our patrol. Right after the maneuvers our company was directed to report to Camp Leonard Wood in Missouri. This happened around the end of May 1941.

We moved into brand new army barracks and received some brand new clothes that actually fit. One-week furloughs were given to the men that asked for them. I wanted to go, but I had no way to get home. Most of the guys from Ohio stayed in camp. The 22nd Ordnance Company's function was to inspect, repair and resupply all fighting units with their firearms, rifles, machine guns, handguns, artillery cannons, and all types of field instruments or anything that fired a bullet or a shell. The company was equipped with bus-like trucks containing gun parts, workbenches, a full machine shop, a small foundry and all types of transport vehicles. The company was divided into five different working sections; small arms, artillery, instruments, machine shop and automotive.

I was placed into the small arms section. I learned how to disassemble all kinds of guns, name the parts, learn their function and put them back together again. Since I was somewhat mechanically inclined, this was very easy for me. I liked my job and I got pretty good at what I did. Soon, they made me the leader of the small arms group. I also worked on the firing range helping the soldiers learn to shoot at targets. I was assigned a small truck to carry my tools and drive from our camp shop to the firing range. Most of the range firing took place during the morning hours three or four times per week. I always took another man with me; most of the time it was Ralph Clark. We became good friends.

This part of my service was almost like any other job. We got up at 5:30 A.M. After roll call we had breakfast and then got in our trucks and went to our assigned tasks. After dinner we were free to go to the PX, go

Alex Kunevicius working on an Army issue 1903 Springfield rifle, Fort Leonard Wood, Missouri, July 1941.

to the post USO or stay in the barracks and write letters, etc. It was lights out at 9:00 P.M. Fort Leonard Wood was in the state of Missouri, eight miles off Highway Route 66, about 120 miles from St. Louis, 75 miles from Springfield and about 15 miles from the town of Rolla. None of these places was easy to get to if you didn't have a car. When the men received weekend passes, they hitchhiked. Once you got to Route 66, which was an eight mile walk from camp, the good people of Missouri picked you up. The two best places for the soldiers to get to were St. Louis and Springfield. The men in the company got to know each other and made friends. Men from Ohio, especially the Cleveland area, fell into special groups for me: Joe Bargiel, John Balog, Art Boessneck, James Bertie, Sid Garett, Peter Scasney, Bill Christopher and Edward Kost just to name a few. As the months went by, the company became a close-knit family. I felt very comfortable being a soldier in the 22nd Ordnance Company. I liked my job since I liked working on the guns, and I liked the men I served with as well.

The barracks we lived in were brand new. My bunk was on the second floor, the second bunk from the wall next to a window. James Bertie had

1. A Letter from the President

the bunk right next to mine. Art Boessneck's bunk was across from mine. Joe Bargiel and Bill Christopher were on the same floor. In the evening we played cards, wrote letters or went to the PX to buy something we needed. A carton of cigarettes sold for $1.50 in the PX. The company had a recreation hall where we played ping pong and other games or just gathered to

James Bertie, Alex Kunevicius, Ralph Clark, Fort Leonard Wood, Missouri, 1941.

do some talking. At the post USO there were many social activities. Dances were very popular, especially when the women's organizations brought in young girls. At a USO-sponsored one-act play writing contest, I wrote a play called "Lights Out," a comedy about what soldiers do after lights are out at the barracks. I won the contest.

On the post at another company two men contacted me about the play. They were from New York, both playwrights. I can't remember their names. They asked me if I would come to New York after my one year of service was over and join them. I thought that was a compliment, but I was never able to see the play acted and never saw the two men again. This happened in late November 1941.

On one occasion, as I was hitchhiking back to camp from Springfield, Missouri, on Route 66 I was picked up by a very nice older couple. They were extremely talkative and friendly and were very interested in me, my background, etc. Since it was dark and somewhat late in the evening, they drove me into the camp to my company area. They told me they lived not too far from the camp and it was no problem to take me back to camp. I thanked them a hundred times.

On Thanksgiving Day, my friend James Bertie and I were playing ping-pong in the recreation room when our first sergeant came in, called my name, and told me there was a man there looking for me. He was followed by a man wearing a badge and a gun on his hip. The man was smiling and he stuck out his hand toward me. He was a sheriff. I froze. He asked me if I remembered about a month ago, he and his wife picked me up hitchhiking from Springfield. I remembered. What a surprise! They drove me back to camp, all the way to our company area. He wanted to know if I would care to have Thanksgiving dinner with him and his wife. He would drive me and a friend to his home and after dinner bring us back again. I looked at the first sergeant. He told us we could go. Both of us could go.

Jim Bertie and I had the nicest dinner at the sheriff's home. His wife was an excellent cook. After dinner was over, she played the piano and sang some hymns for us. As the sheriff was preparing to drive us back to camp, we were saying our good-byes. I felt a very motherly love that very instant. I thanked her and kissed her hand. I never forgot that couple. The people in Missouri were very good people.

2.

December 7, 1941: Trip to the Sea

    I didn't know that much about John Turulis, whose bunk was on my floor. I did not even know what state he came from. I think he was from Chicago, Illinois. He was a loner. He told many different stories about himself, some of them being very hard to believe. He said he owned a gold or silver mine somewhere in the west. He even showed pictures of himself standing in some sort of hole, with his big shovel in his hands and a big western hat on his head. Most of the fellows laughed at his stories and thought he was a nut, but I believed him. He was the only guy in our company that had a car. It was 1938 Auburn four-door sedan. For some reason John trusted me. On a number of occasions I got to drive his car; and one such occasion was marked by history. It was early December of 1941. James Bertie and I had a weekend pass and we were going to go to Springfield to a tavern we visited several times. It was a nice place to meet girls, dance and have a few drinks.

    John Turulis asked James Bertie and me if we would rather go to St. Louis with him. He suggested that we spend some time in St. Louis and then go to East St. Louis to visit some friends he knew. It sounded like it could be fun. John didn't have the personality you wanted to go out girl hunting with, but riding in a car was better than hitchhiking and it really didn't matter where you went — Springfield, Jefferson City, St. Louis or any other town — the only thing that mattered was that you were away from camp for a short time and were able to do as you please. A beautiful drive on old Route 66 through the Ozark Mountains was worth the three and a half hour ride to St. Louis. For some reason that Saturday evening in St. Louis was very dull. It was very quiet everywhere we went. The taverns were unusually empty for a Saturday night. The city closed down everything that was normally open until midnight and even pulled in its sidewalks. We had to get out of there.

John drove over a large bridge which stretched across the Mississippi River into East St. Louis. From here on, for the first time in my life, my memory lapsed. I remember meeting some people in their home. I remember a man's voice saying something about the wine we were drinking being "dandelion wine." I was not a wine drinker. I didn't even know you could make wine out of dandelions, but apparently that is what I was drinking; and then everything went blank. When I opened my eyes it was daylight. I was curled up lying on the back seat of the car. James Bertie was in the front passenger seat sound asleep. John was in the driver's seat sleeping with his head on the steering wheel. I called both their names and got out of the car. The car was off the road, stopped and parked on a grassy slope close to a ditch off a dirt road. In the distance I could see a barn and a farmhouse.

Jim got out of the car and said something like "Where in the hell are we and how did we get here?" We tried to wake up John, but he was out cold. Jim and I managed to get him out of the driver's seat and into the back seat of the car. John murmured a few words and curled up on the seat.

A man carrying a rifle or a shotgun was walking up the road toward us. When he reached us, he wanted to know what are we were doing there and if we were lost. I told him that we were lost and asked where we were. I also told him that the guy that drove us there was sleeping and that we couldn't wake him up. The friendly farmer walked a little closer and informed us that we were 30 minutes southwest of St. Louis, two miles from Route 66. He wanted to know where we were heading, and we told him we were going back to camp at Fort Leonard Wood, Missouri. Our instructions from the farmer were to turn the car around and go the other way. He pointed with his hand and said that when we get to the highway to turn left. We were about 90 miles from camp. I thanked the farmer and gave him a military salute. He picked up his arm in a good-bye gesture.

Jim and I got into the car and turned it around with no problem. We headed in the direction the farmer had advised. In a few minutes we were at Route 66 as the farmer told us. I turned left onto the highway and looked at the gas gauge. The gas tank was half full, enough to get us to camp. Jim mentioned that he hoped it was Sunday. If not, our asses would have been mud. I had hoped it was Sunday too because we were about three hours away from camp. I looked at my watch; it was about 2:15 P.M.

2. December 7, 1941

We were riding for about two hours. It was very quiet. The car radio gave out some country music but mostly static. Jim asked if I had any of that wine the night before. I told him I had. Jim wanted to know what the hell was in that wine! I said to Jim that it was dandelions. The man did say it was dandelions. John Turulis woke up. According to John, in St. Louis all evening we drank beer and then some wine. Later John's friend and he helped me into the back seat of the car where I went out like a light. John remembered leaving his friend's house at daybreak and driving over the Mississippi River Bridge. He could not remember how or when I took over driving the car. We told him about the friendly farmer. Again Jim asked about what the hell was in that wine! John went back to sleep.

About an hour or so later I stopped at a country roadside store to get some pop or something to drink. When I walked into the store, the lady clerk walked up very closely to me, put her hand on my shoulder and started talking about us poor soldiers and how she felt so bad about what happened, and how she was going to do a lot of praying for all of us men. I was shocked and wondered what we did to cause this reaction! I remember just looking into her eyes. Quickly the woman sensed that I didn't know what this was about. Then she spilled the news that the Japanese bombed Pearl Harbor earlier that morning. She told us of how they killed our sailors and soldiers, and that they sank our ships. This was war. She said that it was all over the radio. The woman kept on talking, but I was not listening. I was stunned. War? Japanese? Pearl Harbor? I didn't even know where Pearl Harbor was.

I got three bottles of pop, walked out to the car, and told my friends to turn on the radio. I told them that the Japanese bombed Pearl Harbor just that morning and that we were at war. John jumped in the driver's seat. It was a little after five in the evening, and we were about 20 minutes from camp. Jim was trying to get something on the radio other than country music and static. He finally tuned to a station where a man's voice kept repeating that Pearl Harbor had been bombed, the Japanese attacked us, and something about the fact that President Roosevelt would speak or had already spoken regarding the matter and issued a back to base alert for all military personnel on leave. As we approached the camp entrance gate, it seemed as though there were more military police there than usual, but the camp was quiet.

When we got to our company area, some of our men were walking back to the barracks from the mess hall after dinner. In the barracks the men had their radios on. I soon found out that Pearl Harbor was in Hawaii in the blue Pacific. First Sergeant Van Meter walked through the barracks proclaiming that all leaves were cancelled. The company commander, Captain William Coyle, would talk to us the next morning. The entire camp was now on war footing.

Almost instantly the barracks were filled with rumors. Someone was saying that he heard we were going to go to California, the Japanese were going to attack the West Coast, and that's where we were going to go ... to California. There were more rumors and some men became instant war strategists. Someone proclaimed that Japan was a country of small islands. A lot of men confidently spoke up that our guys were going to kick their asses by Christmas. Geography was one of my favorite subjects in high school. I knew the blue Pacific Ocean was an enormous body of water about one-third of the earth's circumference. I knew it was going to take us a long time to get to Japan, especially if we had to fight the Japanese to get there.

The next morning when daybreak came roll call was taken and our company commander, Captain Coyle, spoke to us. He told us our company was now on war alert. All leaves were cancelled until further notice. He suggested we make our calls or write letters home and straighten out our personal affairs. Captain Coyle stopped talking for a short while. The lanky Texan seemed to be very emotional. He began telling us how he knew each one of us men would like to get home one more time. He wanted us to know that if at all possible, he would make sure we all got that chance. The men shouted in celebration!

During the next few weeks the camp became a beehive of activity. It seemed there were more and more convoys through camp, troops in full gear, going someplace. It became almost impossible to get to a pay telephone at the PX. The lines were very long. Several medical inspections followed, one after another: short arm inspection (army men know what that is) and the other shots in the arm. Our company's daily activities became more intensified. I still worked at the firing range in the mornings and in the afternoon I worked at our ordnance repair building. The building was located at the edge of the camp across from a railroad track. The building was about 10 to 12 thousand square feet of work space. The small arms department shared this space with the artillery repair department and with the field instrument department. Almost overnight our small arms work space was overtaken with pallets and more pallets filled with

2. December 7, 1941

rifles, machine guns and handguns. Our job was to inspect and repair, if need be, every weapon making sure it was in good working order. An ordnance supply company picked up the inspected firearms and dropped off a new supply of pieces for us to work on.

Our small arms repair group became excellent in what we did. This particular exercise was like a college education in gun repair. We could do it blindfolded. I even had dreams that I was fixing guns. Time was flying by. Christmas was about a week away. Captain Coyle spoke to us again, and he sounded more like a father talking to his children than a company commander talking to his soldiers. He said that he was sorry that none of us men were going to go home for Christmas. As of then, the 22nd Ordnance Company was standing on military travel alert. He made sure we understood that we would be leaving Camp Leonard Wood any day. He stopped talking for a moment then started up again in a strong, manly voice to tell us that if we were still there, we were going to have a very good Christmas, all of us together.

Our company area was about 10 to 15 minutes walking time from the center of our camp headquarters, recreation center and church. The Catholics used the church to celebrate the Holy Mass and the Protestants and Jews used it for their own religious services. My parents and the priest at the Jesuit High School I graduated from instilled in me a strong duty to attend Sunday Mass. I tried to get to church as often as I could to fulfill that obligation. The camp chaplain was a very nice man, a good priest and a very good speaker; however, most of the time he spoke to a half-empty church. After December 7 a miracle happened. The Sunday Mass at the camp church was filled to capacity, and on Christmas morning the church was crammed so full some of the men had to stand outside because there was no room for them in the inn (inside the church, that is).

Captain Coyle kept his word. We did have a nice Christmas. A large, beautiful tree was decorated with some military ornaments giving our recreation room a real Christmas atmosphere. Some of the men filled out Christmas cards and hung them on the tree. Our Christmas dinner was attended by all of our officers and sergeants. The company commander said a prayer and wished everyone a merry Christmas. The mess sergeant and the company cooks outdid themselves. Turkey and ham, sweet potatoes and all kinds of vegetables and rolls filled the mess hall tables. The men ate, talked and laughed and then finished the feast with apple and pumpkin pies. How much better could it be?

585 Raids and Counting

It was about a week after the New Year, in January 1942, that it became apparent we were leaving Camp Leonard Wood, Missouri. Our first order was to deliver to the railroad tracks all of our heavy trucks, bin trucks, parts carriers, tool carriers, small weapons carriers and anything else on wheels our company used to perform the duties we were assigned. At the railroad tracks our equipment was loaded and tied down onto flatbed railroad cars. Someone asked the trainmen where the train was headed but they received no answer. The men were told to empty their footlockers of all their clothes and personal needs into their newly-issued dark blue barracks bags. We were issued new shoes and some dark colored underwear. Again, rumors were flying all over the place. A few of the top rumormongers had us going to California. "That's where our trucks went, California, and that's the place where we are going," they said. My good friend Joe Bargiel, the crown prince of rumormongers, had it almost right. He said, "I heard we were going to some camp in Pennsylvania and there we will wait for further orders."

A few days later we boarded a train, and in about a one-day ride we got off the train in Indian Town Gap, Pennsylvania. This was truly an army camp of debarkation. Trainload after trainload of guys filled the camp, coming into the camp and going out of the camp. Our company stayed here four or five days. Since this camp was not too far from Reading and Harrisburg, Pennsylvania, some men got permission to go into those towns to say good-bye to their parents, wives, and sweethearts who came there for that occasion. I managed to get a phone to call home. My parents wanted to know where I was going. I told them I didn't know. It wasn't easy to say good-bye. My mother and father took the good-byes very hard. Lights went on in the barracks about 3:00 in the morning. A sergeant came in shouting, "Up and at it, roll call in 15 minutes." He ran through the sleeping solders' quarters. Everyone jumped.

At roll call we were told we were leaving the camp that morning. After a very early breakfast and a short break, we got into trucks and busses for a short ride to the railroad area. It was barely daybreak, but we could see the long train, maybe 15 or 20 cars or more, and we were not the only ones on the move. At least a thousand soldiers lined the waiting platform ready to board the train. Carrying our barracks bags we got on the train. It was crowded, but we got into our seats with the barracks bags under our feet. The train ride from Indian Town Gap to the Brooklyn port and shipyards didn't seem that long.

2. December 7, 1941

That very same day, by mid-afternoon, in a single-file line up the gangplank the solders carrying their bags boarded the good steamship *Thomas Berry*. When our turn came, we walked up the gangplank onto the ship. The ship's crewmen directed us to our quarters. Apparently the ship was pretty much filled with soldiers. We walked down and down several flights of stairs to a large area filled with bunks erected four deep on top of each other. A very small place at each bunk was designated for your bag. There was a blanket on each bunk and to make matters worse workers were still welding some of the bunks in place. Someone hollered, "We're down in the hole." With my parents I had crossed the Atlantic Ocean four times on passenger ships before my 18th birthday. I remembered the fancy staterooms, the beautiful dining rooms and lounge areas. What I was looking at then was not going to be a luxury trip to wherever we were going.

Our company was directed to one side of this large area and we took up the bunks next to the ship's outer wall. There was a life jacket on every bunk. We were told to wear it or carry it at all times. I lucked out. My bunk was the second bunk, about four feet from the floor on the aisle-side next to the wall. There were no portholes. I believe we were either below or just above the ship's waterline. A severe draft flowed through the entire area, and it was cold. The men flung their barracks bags on their bunks and started moving around. Whoever designed the men's room, the latrine, must not have had the men's modesty in mind. It must have been far, far back in his mind. In an adjoining open room about 20 white toilets, about one foot apart, lined one long side of the wall. On the other side of the room, a long trough that looked like a rain gutter slightly slanted to make the urine flow downhill into the sewer pipe. A fixed water flow was constantly on. Right around the corner from this fabulous restroom was a wall lined with sinks, a place to brush your teeth and shave with hot or cold saltwater. There were no mirrors on the wall.

I believe we were among the last troops to board the ship. Very soon after we were assigned to our living-sleeping quarters, First Sergeant Van Meter shouted at us to get our attention. He said, "I just received some information. Listen. The ship will leave the port this afternoon at 18 hundred hours. We will be allowed to go up on deck, but now a chow line is forming on 'H' deck. Let's eat." We had to go up several flights to get to "H" deck, and when we saw the chow line, it was a mile long. You could not see the end of the line. If it wasn't for the ship's crewmen directing traffic, we probably would not have ever found the end of the line. Some-

585 Raids and Counting

one said there were going to be 4,500 troops on board this ship. I thought they were all in the chow line at the same time. As we approached the entrance to the mess hall, the line split into two directions around the food serving area. There were no menus to look at and it took only about ten seconds to go through the serving line. Nobody asked you what you wanted. The ship's food handlers handed each soldier an already filled metal tray with some stew, mashed potatoes, peas, a piece of bread, a slice of cake and a cup of coffee. There were no seats to sit on. Long tables about waist high were where you stood and ate your food.

Over the loudspeaker a voice kept repeating, "When you are done eating, empty your tray of any leftovers in the designated cans, place the trays on the racks and leave the mess hall." It didn't take our group very long to eat. When we were finished we did exactly what the announcer told us to do and the left the mess hall.

Passageways and stairways were almost impossible to get through. Some soldiers, still carrying their duffle bags, were being directed by the ship's crewmen to their sleeping quarters. Some of the soldiers were just standing there, looking around, possibly separated from their companies or just lost. Since we were allowed to go up on deck, I joined a group of our guys working their way up the crowded stairs. When we got to the outside deck, it was also very crowded.

In time I managed to work my way to the port (left) side of the ship and a place at the ship's rail. When I looked down on the pier, the ship's gangplanks were already removed from the pier into the ship. Maybe a dozen or so men were walking around, some of them doing something with the ropes holding the ship in place. I could see the ship slowly moving away from the pier. The ship became alive. A very loud blast on the ship's horn told all of us that we were leaving the United States. Some of the guys had tears in their eyes and some lifted their arms as if waving goodbye to someone they left behind. On the pier there were no people waving their handkerchiefs or flags wishing us a happy voyage. There were no bands playing one of the John Philip Sousa marches to victory. There were no beautiful girls there throwing kisses at their departing lovers.

I stayed on deck for a long time hugging the ship's railing and watching the city's lights glowing in the distance. I thought of my father and mother and sister and said a prayer, and I somehow knew in my heart that someday I would come back to them again. It was getting very dark and it was very cold. When we got back down to our sleeping quarters, some

2. December 7, 1941

of the men called it "the hole" because of lack of something to do. We were huddled in our bunks fully dressed, shoes and all. The place was dimly lit, and it was very cold. A strong breeze flowed through the entire area. Somewhere, something had to be opened to the outside to cause this very uncomfortable condition. I recall most of the activity was in the latrine and washroom, men standing around talking and smoking cigarettes.

"Where are we going?" was the question that came from everyone's lips. Master Sergeant Bridwell told us our destination was not yet revealed to anyone. He said, "I don't think our company commander, Captain Coyles, knows yet." Sergeant Bridwell was always straight with us. Everybody liked him and believed him. I crawled into my bunk with my clothes on, put the life jacket under my head and pulled on the blankets. "Could it get any worse?" I thought. This accommodation had to be the bottom of the barrel. There was a creaking sound, and I could hear water splashing against the ship. I could feel the ship's slight rocking motion and hear the ship's engines filling the place with a humming sound. I couldn't sleep so I just listened and listened.

The sounds of a navy-type whistle, a high note, a higher note and a lower note, ended the night's sleeping. The men took their turns in the latrine and the washbasins. Somehow there seemed to be order, military order. When our company's turn came to have breakfast, the line seemed shorter. This time we each picked up a clean tray and carried it through the chow line. Scrambled eggs, sausage, hash brown potatoes, toast and coffee as well as orange juice was the breakfast of the morning.

We were told First Sergeant Van Meter was going to hold an orientation talk soon after breakfast and everyone must attend. Sergeant Van Meter was a regular army man. He was a southern boy. He did not waste time on long conversations and he was always to the point. He said, "This is what I got from our company commander, Captain Coyle. No company formation will take place while we are aboard the ship. Wake up call will be at 5:30 A.M. Keep your assigned sleeping area as clean as possible. Two meals will be served each day, breakfast and dinner, at the times posted in the mess hall. Don't forget to eat. A bar of saltwater soap will be issued to everyone so you can take a saltwater shower anytime you want. Don't forget to take one. You can go up on deck any time you want to. Wear or carry your life jacket at all times. Try to attend all of the ship's activities. We are not alone. There are 4,250 men and women on board this ship. Don't listen to rumors. Nobody knows where this ship is going. Company dismissed."

The words "company dismissed" meant we were now on our own. I asked my friend Jim Bertie if he wanted to go up on deck. He said, "Let's go." To get to the top deck we had to walk up four flights of narrow metal steps. Men going up or men coming down had to step sideways to squeeze by one another. Two flights up was "H" Deck, the big mess hall. Men were still in line waiting to have their breakfast. When we got by the chow line floor, the going was easier and we finally got to the outside decks where a strong, cold wind made us grab onto the outside sidewall railings. We were at the bow (front end) of the ship. On deck men were milling around. Some were pointing fingers at something. I looked on the starboard (right) side of the ship and five or six miles away you could see land. We were traveling along the U.S. coastline. The morning sun behind some light clouds was on the port side of the ship in the east. The ship was going south. The big question was, "Where are we going?" Some of the war strategists said, "This doesn't make sense. If we were going to Europe to fight Hitler the ship should be going north then across the Atlantic." Some smart guys mentioned Cuba, some of the Caribbean Islands and even Brazil. There were German subs in the Atlantic. A large gun turret was mounted quite high at the bow of the ship equipped, with two side-by-side mounted 20 millimeter machine guns, the kind mainly used against anti-aircraft attacks. Three men were in the turret ready to man the guns.

Very soon the deck was filled with men looking for a place to sit. There were no lounge chairs on deck. Some of the men were climbing a staircase to the upper deck. Jim Bertie and I followed. The upper deck had a large view to both sides of the ship and the front. The upper deck became the prime seating area. You sat on your life jackets or your bunk blanket. It was windy and cold, but most of the men with their coats on stayed on deck. It seemed nobody wanted to go back down to the hole. Jim and I stayed on deck until it was time to eat our second meal of the day. The chow line was more orderly than it had been the previous day, but the food didn't change much. We carried the tray through the line. It was stew, potatoes, a vegetable, a piece of some kind of pie and a cup of coffee. Most of the guys gulped the food down in a few minutes standing at the tables. Some guys tried to pretend they were feasting at a fancy restaurant, but it took me about ten minutes to down my second meal of the day. At the mess hall exit on the wall as a hand-printed sign: "Non-denominational services will be held this evening in the mess hall at 8:00 P.M. Everybody is welcome." At home I attended church every Sunday. I

2. December 7, 1941

liked to listen to a good sermon, especially if the priest was a good speaker. I was going to try to attend this service for sure.

At my bunk, out of my duffle bag, I pulled out a paperback book I picked up on the train. It was impossible to sit on the bunk and read. The top bunk was too low; there was no clearance for your head. Lying down with my head on my life jacket, I had to stick the book out to the edge of the bunk to get some light to see the print. I read for awhile. No wonder someone left this book on the train, it was full of some guys who lived in the east in a big city who decided to go west to live on a cattle ranch. It was boring, but there was one good thing about the story, it put me to sleep. I left that book on top of my bunk hoping someone would pick it up, but nobody ever did.

That evening I joined at least a dozen of our guys to go to the 8:00 P.M. service. When we got to the mess hall the food handlers were still cleaning up the place. Two men were pushing a small organ to one side of what must have been the front part of the hall. The hall filled up very quickly. Everybody was standing around the tables. There was no place to sit down. Soon an army captain and a sergeant appeared at the front at the hall. Somebody hollered "attention" and the sergeant said "at ease" almost at the same time. The captain was an army Protestant minister. He lifted both of his arms up in a very peaceful sign. The sergeant sat down at the organ and started playing it to get the men's attention. The hall became very quiet; all you heard was the music. The captain introduced himself as Captain Frank Bauer, an army chaplain. He said a short prayer. He asked God to bless all the men and women on this ship. He asked God to bless our families, our loved ones and our friends. He said God chose us for this saintly mission; it is history in the making. When he stopped praying, the sergeant played the organ again and led the men in singing some hymns, some of them from World War I and then the chaplain spoke again for about a half hour or more. This speech was not the fire and brimstone type of speech, but one of sacrifice and love, love of our neighbor, duty to our country and why we were there. When he spoke about love of family, girlfriends and wives some of the guys had tears in their eyes. The chaplain was a pretty good speaker; he even had the men laughing several times. When he was done speaking, the sergeant led the men in singing one more hymn and the service was over. The chaplain blessed the men again and bid everyone a good night. I think all the men there had a warm feeling about the evening service.

Next morning I woke up before the wake-up call whistle blew. The perpetual cold breeze that flowed throughout the sleeping quarters did not seem to be as cold. I thought this was a good time to try the saltwater shower. For my first time I think I did pretty well. Trying to get the lather from the saltwater soap was a job, partly real and partly intriguing. Perhaps the next time I would get more lather from the soap; this time all I could say with any certainty is "I got wet. I took a shower this morning."

We were told to keep our sleeping area clean and orderly. All you had to do to keep it orderly was fold your blanket and place it on your bunk. Most the guys did that pretty well. After a fast scrambled eggs, home fries, sausage and toast breakfast some of my buddies and I hurried up to the outer deck. The big surprise of the day was the weather. The wind was still strong, still blowing, but it was not as cold; it was almost warm and very pleasant. The morning sun was shining brightly, climbing up into an almost cloudless sky. Most of the guys took off their coats or jackets and a few sun worshippers stripped themselves down to the waist. We climbed to the upper deck to try and find a better place to sit down. The land on the right side of the ship was still there, but barely visible. It looked like we were going farther out to sea, but the ship was still sailing south.

That day, by midmorning, everybody on board somehow knew the ship was sailing along the Georgia-Florida coastline. That very afternoon the big alert, like a great news flash on the radio, was that somebody leaked a bombshell. In seconds it spread throughout the ship. This was not a rumor; this was the real thing. It was, "We are headed to the Caribbean to the Panama Canal and the blue Pacific." Nobody seemed to know how this information got started. Perhaps somebody from the upper echelon leaked it intentionally. Everybody on board accepted it as fact. It wasn't long before the rumors started. The one I thought might have some merit was that we were going to the Philippines to help General McArthur. Of course, we had no way of knowing if he was still there or not. The one that also made some sense was, "We're going to Hawaii to reinforce the army garrison there before the Japanese decide to invade the islands." Hawaii was nice, I thought. I had never been there. The paradise islands of the Pacific, the hula girls; that is the place for me. I think I forgot about the war.

That evening, and every evening thereafter, there were services of one kind or another; it didn't matter whether or not you were Protestant, Catholic or Jew; everybody went to the services. There was some singing,

2. December 7, 1941

some talking and it made the evening more interesting. The warmer weather also changed the men's evening and nightly activities. A lot of the men carried their blankets to the deck and bedded down there. Your life jacket was your pillow and your blanket under or over you made a comfortable bed, or at least that's what everybody said. In time, the U.S. shoreline disappeared. Here and there an island would appear on one side of the ship and sometimes the other side. With the men, it became a guessing game, "What island is it? Is that Cuba, or is that Jamaica?" The ship was now sailing southwest. At times we saw small fishing or pleasure boats not too far in the distance. I often wondered why whoever was in charge of the ship did not say something about what islands we were going by or where we were or verified where we were going. Then the islands disappeared. We were in the open sea. If we were going to the Panama Canal, we had to be in the open part of the Caribbean Sea with only clear water everywhere.

One morning during our voyage we approached land. The sun was hot; the men filled the upper decks. Men on small boats and tugs were waving at us from shore and we leaned over the ship's railings to wave back. "Where in the hell are we?" everyone wanted to know. As if with the answer to the question, the ship's loudspeaker came on with a message, "We are now on the Atlantic side of the entrance to the Panama Canal. The Panama Canal is a ship canal that joins the Atlantic Ocean to the Pacific Ocean. To get to the Pacific side of the canal we will travel through the Gatun Locks, the Gatun Lake, the Madden Lake and the Miraflores locks. Each lock is 1,000 feet long and 115 feet wide. The length of the entire canal system is about 50 miles. On the other side of the canal the ship will make a stop in Balboa to take on fuel. The journey will take us all day subject to our turn at the locks. Enjoy the trip."

A little bit of the engineering marvel of this canal might be of interest to some. From the Atlantic side of the ship, we entered the first of the three Gatun locks. Water flows from Gatun Lake and fills the lock, lifting the ship to the next lock level. A locomotive type unit on both sides of the lock pulls the ship through the next two locks using the same water lift procedure. From the third lock, the ship enters Gatun Lake, the highest point of the canal. Gatun Lake is the longest part of the canal, narrow in places, dotted with tiny overgrown islands with a very jungle-like shoreline, beautiful to look at. From Gatun Lake on the way down to the Pacific Ocean, the ship entered the first lock, named Pedro Miguel. The lock emptied its water, lowering the ship to the Lake Miraflores level. Two more locks brought the ship down to the Pacific Ocean and the Port of Balboa.

While the ship stopped in Balboa to refuel I got a chance to get off the ship. Somehow I got on a work detail loading boxes and boxes of fruit and vegetables onto the ship. Getting off the ship was a big deal. At least I got to say I stepped foot in the Balboa District of Panama City, Panama. The work details ended as it started to get dark. The pier's floodlight lit up the dock and the ship's decks. The guys were milling around the decks waiting to see the ship leave Balboa. There were no evening services scheduled of any kind. I think it was Sid Garrett, Joe Bargiel, Jim Bertie and I up on the loft we found above the upper deck, out of the way, overlooking the two lower decks. This was a very good place to sit and observe everything that was going on below. The ship was still taking on fuel. The breeze was so warm and pleasant on your face it could put you to sleep, and then it was very quiet.

When I opened my eyes I could see nothing but water on all sides of the ship. From behind the ship the rising run laid a blanket of rays on the water. The water in front of the ship looked like glass, changing color from orange to red to purple. It was beautiful. I never saw anything like it in all of my life. There was no land to be seen anywhere. We were out to sea on the vast Pacific Ocean. Joe Bargiel was awake and sitting nearby smoking a cigarette. He said, "We have some nutty guy driving the ship. He goes left for about ten minutes, and then he goes right for ten minutes. He can't keep this ship sailing in a straight line." Joe was partially right. The ship was zigzagging but for a good reason. This was a method used by ships as an anti-submarine diversion tactic. We later learned every zig and every zag had a different time limit and even that time limit was changed constantly. The ship's crewmen assigned as submarine spotters with field glasses in hand were stationed at all sides of the ship. Gun crews occupied the gun turrets at all times. This ship was in a war setting.

Officers and nurses on board occupied the cabins and decks at the highest level of the ship. For some unexplained military reason the officers had very little contact with the draftees and enlisted men. At times a first or second lieutenant would appear in the mess hall and watch the men going through the chow line. This was not really a great line of duty. The sergeants pretty much had control of their men. Each day got hotter and hotter. Time was measured by what you had to do. The days' greatest

2. December 7, 1941

activity for the men was going through the chow line for breakfast and dinner, taking a saltwater shower, taking care of their personal needs and finding a good spot on deck to look at the beautiful Pacific. Sometimes a group of porpoises put on a classic show for hours, performing their long jumps, swimming and keeping up with the ship. There was hardly any activity in the men's sleeping quarters. Nobody slept there, it was all on deck. On deck the men gathered in groups mainly from the same companies, friends helping each other if need be. The amazing part of this voyage was that for the large number of men on board this ship, I never saw or heard of any problems among the men of any kind. Perhaps it was because we were all in the same boat.

From the ship's crew, from the men that traveled the seas constantly, we learned one thing: how to do our laundry in saltwater without a washing machine. At the very end of the ship, the stern, at the very lowest deck, you are closest to the ship's wake or the track left in the water by the moving ship. Here you string a thin, long rope through your dirty clothes, tie a knot and throw the bundle overboard into the wake for about ten minutes, watch it jump up and down in the wake, pull the bundle up and dry the clean clothes in the hot sun. I thought this might come in handy some day on our future cruises.

The evening non-denominational services were attended by most of the men. The army ministers kept the events interesting with talks, men singing hymns, and popular songs. The religious services were performed on deck every Saturday and Sunday. During the day smoking was allowed anywhere on the ship. At night there was no smoking on deck and no lights of any kind. The decks were dark for an obvious reason: submarines.

On the third day out of Panama we crossed the equator. The news came over the ship's loudspeaker and it was a shock to some of the guys. Apparently we were not going to Hawaii or the Philippines as some of the men thought we were. Even though the ship was traveling southwest, the Philippines or Hawaii was our destination according to the rumor mongers. That rumor died instantly.

As we crossed the equator the ship's crewmen performed some sort of ceremony for the men, an old sailor's tradition that called for dousing some with water as a blessing for crossing the line into the other side of the world, the bottom side. It became a festive day. The crewmen carried on their activities on all the outside decks most of the day. Several of the ship's officers walked among the men explaining the day's ritual. At our second meal, each man received a candy bar and a bottle of soda pop. I think I received a Clark chocolate bar. That evening the conversation about where we were going changed. Going southwest on the vast Pacific, the ship was 10,000 miles from everywhere. The days and the time started to roll together. Is this the fifth day after the equator or the tenth day? Someone would ask and no one would answer.

James Bertie was not a great talker. He liked to read and wrote notes about the day's activities. Maybe that's why he was one of my best buddies. I did most of the talking and he did most of the listening. This day he and I had a nice shady spot to sit in on deck. He told me about a movie he saw or he read somewhere about this famous artist who went to a Pacific tropical island to live the easy life. He shacked up with a beautiful young native girl, drank wine, and painted pictures. He couldn't remember his name but thought it was a true story. This guy was a lover; what a nice way to go. I assured Jim that that's exactly what the generals had in mind for us, and made a wish, hoping that type of life would happen to both of us.

Some days were more interesting than others. A group of our guys was in the breakfast chow line when First Sergeant Russell Van Meter came by with a message and asked the guys to pass it on. He said, "Lieutenant Benjamin Rabin volunteered to climb up into the crow's nest as a submarine spotter. He is going up there this morning. Get up on deck and give him a hand. Cheer him on." Lieutenant Rabin was in charge of the small arms repair section I was in. I knew him pretty well, and I liked him. He was the lieutenant that assigned me to do the rifle repairs at the firing range at Camp Leonard Wood. He was pretty handy with tools. He was a chemical engineer in civilian life and his home state was Kentucky. When we got to the deck and looked up, a man was climbing down the ladder from the crow's nest. The crow's nest was 35 to 50 feet high in the ship's forward mast. Lieutenant Rabin was standing there with a man who seemed to be giving him some instructions. The man climbed down the ladder, saluted the two men at the bottom of the mast and walked away.

When Lieutenant Rabin started up the ladder our guys gave him a supporting shout, "Be careful, Lieutenant" and some applause. About halfway up the ladder, his one foot slipped off the ladder rung, but he caught himself. Everyone went "oooh, oooh." I think he did it purposely to give everybody a little show. Lieutenant Rabin continued to pull a two hour submarine watch in the crow's nest every day. He was asked to

2. December 7, 1941

Troop ship *Thomas Berry* stops to refuel at Bora Bora Island in the South Pacific. The troops onboard enjoyed the scenic view.

describe what it is like up in the crow's nest. His first comment was, "You have to have a very strong stomach." Even a very slight rock of the ship magnifies movement up on the mast between a five and fifteen degree swing ratio. Not too many men can pull duty in the crow's nest. Lieutenant Benjamin Rabin was one man among not too many men.

James Bertie had it written down in his log. He said it was the 19th day out of Panama when we saw many small fishing and sail boats and in the distance we saw land. We could see men in the small boats waving their arms and small flags at us and we waved back. An announcement came over the loudspeaker. "We are approaching a French Polynesian island named Bora Bora to refuel and take on fresh water. We will be here approximately 12 hours." The message was short, but the day became very interesting. The ship slowly entered a horseshoe type bay surrounded with beautiful palm trees, small native huts and sandy beaches the likes of which I had never seen in my life. This did not look like a harbor; it looked like something we saw in the movies, a tropical paradise. When our ship dropped anchor in the middle of the bay a very large barge moved closer and closer to one side of our ship. With ropes the crewmen pulled the

585 Raids and Counting

barge next to the ship and the two were separated only by the barge's protective soft barriers. Large hoses appeared between the barge and the ship and the fueling began.

Almost immediately the bay filled with small canoes. Young native men and boys jumped into the water waving their arms and asking the men on the ship for coins. The men started to throw nickels, dimes and quarters into the water and the natives were swimming like fish diving for the coins. This went on for most of the day until the men ran out of coins. Some of the natives standing in their canoes pitched fruit up to the men on ship as a message of thank you and friendship. I was not lucky enough to get any. It was getting dark when the fuel barge pulled away from the ship. Almost immediately we heard the ship's anchor being pulled out of the water and the ship starting slowly moving out of the bay. At a short distance on both sides of the ship natives paddling their canoes formed a farewell line and led the ship out into the ocean. It was something to see. Everybody watched until the canoes and the island of Bora Bora disappeared into the dark.

It was on the fifth day out of Bora Bora the ship crossed the International Date Line. On the night before at the scheduled evening meeting, a navy officer gave the men a short history about the line going all the way back to the Magellan expeditions in the 16th century. Apparently Magellan had a problem with Spain about a date on which he returned from one of his trips. This imaginary line in the middle of the Pacific along the 180th degree of longitude offsets the date as one travels east or west across it. Anyone traveling west crossing the line loses one entire day. Going east across the line the traveler gains one entire day. He also mentioned a ceremony that goes with crossing the line the sailors performed on their underlings and added, "You will see that tomorrow. I think you will enjoy it."

The next day on an upper deck the ceremony started with King Neptune sitting on a throne covered with fish nets and surrounded with his court, including Davy Jones and Princess Aphrodite. The ranking seamen, who had crossed the International Date Line before, acted in front of the King's entire court and physically degraded, abused and performed some brutal acts on other seamen who had not yet crossed the line. They were made to wear women's clothes; they were smeared with shaving cream and pelted with mush and raw eggs. The show went on for a good part of the day and at the end by some law of King Neptune the disgraced seamen were proclaimed to have crossed the International Date Line and were ele-

2. December 7, 1941

vated into the Order of the Golden Dragon and all was well on the Pacific. Everyone on board the ship received a paper certificate certifying he or she had crossed the International Date Line.

Jimmy Bertie was never wrong about things he wrote down in his log, but some of the guys were giving him a hard time about how many days we were traveling from one place to another starting from the Brooklyn docks to the Panama Canal. Jim had that trip down at eight days. From the Panama Canal to the equator he listed four days. From the equator to Bora Bora he listed 12 days and from Bora Bora to the International Date Line he listed four days. According to Jim's count we had been sailing the Atlantic and Pacific oceans for 28 days. Some guys marked the calendar to keep track of the days we traveled and some guys just lost count or did not care anymore. The other discussion among the men was how fast the ship was traveling and how many miles we had covered. Since the ship was zig-zagging, the smart estimators had us traveling between 300 and 350 miles per 24 hour period. In 28 days we traveled between 8,400 and 9,800 miles. So where were we going? Everyone really wanted to know.

After we crossed the International Date Line the ship's course never changed. We were still traveling southwest. Rumors were widespread that we were headed for New Zealand or Australia. Maybe that thought was instilled in the men by someone from the upper office, maybe intentionally. Where else could we go? For most of the trip the Pacific Ocean was smooth as glass, but now a few waves appeared and the ship developed a slight rock. Each day the waves got bigger and the ship rocked a little bit more. Some of the guys started missing breakfast and even the second meal of the day. The weather did not change much, it was warm but it became windy. Lieutenant Ben Rabin, who pledged to pull duty in the crow's nest for the entire trip, came down one day and never went up there again. I felt very lucky that the waves did not bother me at all. I considered myself an experienced sea-going man because of my four previous trips across the Atlantic. My last trip from Amsterdam to New York took 14 days. It was December and the Atlantic Ocean was very rough. I was 17 years old. One morning the ocean was so rough my father and I were the only two passengers in the ship's dining room having breakfast.

While in high school, I remember reading or studying about the very rough waters of the Tasmanian Sea located between New Zealand and Australia. We were there! I was sure we were there and each day it got worse. Because of strong winds and rough waters all on-deck activities changed from men basking in the sun to men holding onto their stomachs. A message over the ship's loudspeaker suggested all personnel should move to the inner parts of the ship to their bunk areas. A lot of the bunks were already occupied with men trying to shake the curse that came over them called sea-sickness. Some of the men spent the day running from their bunks to the men's room and unfortunately some of them didn't make it. It was a mess. Too bad they were not issued sick bags. It would have been the right thing to do. My father was a traveler. I learned from him the worst place to be on the ship during rough seas is the very front or back of the ship. Our bunk area was closer to mid-ship. We were lucky, and most of our guys were holding on pretty well. The chow line for breakfast and dinner was getting shorter and shorter, and the mess hall was not as crowded as it used to be.

One evening the presiding minister holding the evening services lasted about ten minutes. "Good God," he said out loud and ran out of the hall. The minister's assistant, the sergeant playing the piano, just kept playing. The men gave him a nice round of applause. We knew the officers on the upper decks were having their problems also. The higher you go on the ship, the longer the rock. A young man sitting on his bunk kept repeating, "God, when are we getting off this ship?" I wished I could help him, but I didn't know the answer to his question either.

It was either the third or fourth day during these rough seas that I managed to sneak out on deck near the exit hatch. I held on to a crossbar because the wind was blowing very hard and the waves were high. There was nobody on deck. The gun turrets up front were empty of gunners and the submarine spotters were not at their posts. Holding onto the crossbar I tried to time the ship's rocking motion. I watched the front end of the ship plunge deep into the water with waves overflowing the deck. For many seconds it seemed like it would never come up again and then, like a giant whale, the front end of the ship rose so high I could not see the water at all. This unwelcome up and down motion repeated itself every 90 seconds or so.

It was unfortunate, but the ship's action divided the guys into two different categories: the guys in their bunks, running to the john, missing every meal and feeling sorry for themselves, and the guys who were not sick, walking around like this too will pass, looking for something to do. This was about a 50–50 split. I fell into the second group with the guys stronger than the wretched sea, opposing the elements, good or bad. Then,

2. December 7, 1941

whether predestined or on purpose, somebody up there rolled the dice and came up with snake eyes. The great disaster struck. That morning, at breakfast, the word got around that the second meal of the day would be cooked turkey, stuffing and all the trimmings just like Thanksgiving. "Why?" Everybody wanted to know. This was the end of February, not November.

Among the guys, a discussion began as to why the ship's command became so generous when during the last four weeks our two daily meals were nothing to brag about; scrambled eggs, hash brown potatoes, toast and coffee for breakfast and a camouflaged stew for dinner. John McGurgan threatened to write a letter to the president about this trip. His uncle was a city councilman or something. John was sure he could get his letter to the president of the United States. I kept thinking about the turkey. I liked turkey, and just thinking about it made my mouth water. I could not wait. My friend Jim said he was going to get a second helping if possible.

The guys had different theories about the turkey dinner and some of the theories were not good. Joe Bargiel had the worst theory of them all. He tried to assure the guys that those turkeys were meant for the officers and nurses on board the ship. Something had gone wrong with the turkeys. They must have been spoiled, he thought! Now they were going to give them to us. Joe was on a mission. He tried to convince the men that he was right. "Don't eat the turkey," he said, "You'll be sorry if you do. I tell you, don't eat the turkey."

That afternoon the guys from my outfit, the 22nd Ordnance Company, got into the chow line just a little earlier than usual. We were hungry. We were standing in line for a feast. At the food counter I asked for and received a piece of dark turkey meat, some stuffing and a sweet potato. We ate the turkey. It was very good. I can't remember if Jim Bertie went for seconds or not, but Joe Bargiel's "don't eat the turkey" suggestion failed; almost everybody I knew had the turkey that day.

That night the sea was still very choppy. It was impossible to find a dry place on deck to sleep. Reluctantly everybody slept in their bunks with their clothes and shoes on. I tried to get comfortable in my bunk and I was having a hard time trying to sleep. About 1:00 A.M. it happened to me. I woke up in a panic. My stomach was telling me I wasn't going to make it to the john. I jumped out of my bunk and ran towards the latrine. There was a traffic jam. Guys from all directions were running to the same place: the men's room. When I got there, there was a long line of men ahead of me. The twenty commodes in the john were occupied. The guys in line were begging the men sitting on the commodes to hurry. That very moment I would have picked hell to being in here at this time. I finally got to a commode. I had dysentery and so did all the other guys on this ship. There was just one man I knew on board not affected: his name was Joe Bargill. I promised myself from then on when Joe told me something, I'd listen. For the next three days the ship became a big floating latrine. Some of the men could not get to the john in time. The commodes overflowed. The crewmen used water hoses in the passageways and on deck to clean the undesirable mess. I'll leave it at that.

3.

Australia

On the third day after the great turkey dinner fiasco, on the starboard side of the ship, in the distance we could see land. For some reason the ship was traveling northwest. How could that be, the guys wondered. Very soon that morning over the ship's loudspeaker came the news all of the men on the good ship *Thomas Berry* were waiting for. We were told to be ready this afternoon to disembark the ship in the port of Melbourne, Australia. The greatest shout I ever heard in all of my life echoed throughout the passageways and decks of the ship, and in sequence, the ship's horns blasted several times. It was Saturday, February 28, 1942. Jim Bertie was fast with his count. He shouted, "We've been sailing on this tub for 38 days. I've got it written down. I will never forget it." I thought to myself, "I'll never forget it either."

Almost immediately our company became a regimented army unit again. First Sergeant Russell Van Meter, with the help of other sergeants, had the guys packing their belongings into their barracks bags, getting ready for the long-awaited departure. On deck, in the distance, we could see the outline of the city of Melbourne, and in a short time the ship docked at a very large pier. The pier was filled with people, busses and trucks. There was an Australian military band playing American military marches. One army group after another walked down the ship's debarkation ramp carrying their barracks bags on their shoulders. Some soldiers dragged their bags behind them, drained of their strength by the rough waters and the turkey incident. The minute the solders touched the ground, they were directed into the trucks and busses and as soon as these were filled, they left the pier.

When our turn came, we walked down the ramp and climbed into the trucks. It was warm. The trucks were uncovered. Along the way, people waved at us and we waved back. Some people with a heavy Australian

585 Raids and Counting

Troops disembarking ship, Melbourne, Australia, February 1942.

3. Australia

accent shouted, "Welcome, Yanks." They seemed very friendly and very glad to see us. After a short ride, the trucks pulled into a place that looked like the city park. We drove by some signs that read "Melbourne Zoo" and then into an open field filled with rows and rows of pyramid army tents. Several older gentlemen with large Australian hats cocked to one side were directing traffic and giving instructions to the soldiers getting out of the trucks. When our company gathered together, our first sergeant told us to occupy the nearby row of tents, five men to a tent. Each tent's floor was covered with eight to ten inches of straw. There was nothing else in the tent, not even bunks. The straw and our one army blanket became the bunk we slept in.

At one end of the tent area, about 50 feet away, a large fenced-in outdoor shower and latrine facility was built for our use. Food was served by cheerful women in a pavilion type building at the other end of the tents. That evening our first meal in Australia was a piece of lamb, potatoes, and a piece of white bread at least two inches thick covered with butter. I'll never forget the way the Aussies fed us that bread. Later in the evening, as we prepared to bed down, an older gentleman told us straw was cool to sleep on in the summer time and warm to sleep on in the winter. He didn't know why, but it was. We slept on the straw that night and it was not bad at all. In the morning we took freshwater showers; what a blessing compared to what we had for the past 38 days. The guys had smiles on their faces again.

Breakfast was served in the large pavilion by friendly Australian men and women. There were long tables and benches to sit on. Such comfort we hadn't experienced for such a long time. There were not as many soldiers here as there were on the ship. This was one, only one, of several places the soldiers from the ship were camped in. Later we found out our camp was one of the nicest; we were lucky. Our company commander and his staff of officers occupied tents in the same row as we did. At formation our company commander, Captain Coyle, told us up until such time as he got his orders, we were free to leave the camp area, go to the nearby zoo, go to town to sightsee, do as we wished but to make sure we found our way back to camp. He thought the park was called Parkville Victoria.

Our stay in Australia lasted for seven days. Almost every soldier there had a story to tell. The Australian people were very friendly. They stopped U.S. soldiers on the street and asked them to come to their homes to have tea. At first they did not want to go for tea but later found out in Australia tea meant a very nice feast. Everyone then wanted to go home to tea. Australians drank their beer warm. The first time Jim Bertie and I walked outside the park a group of U.S. soldiers were standing on a street corner drinking beer out of large liter bottles. When we asked them where they got the beer, they pointed to a small store. Jim and I each got a bottle of beer. The beer was warm. I wasn't much of a beer drinker and a liter of warm beer was more than I could handle. Some guys drank that warm beer until they got smashed and had to have their friends help them back to their camp areas.

Some of the Australian eating habits were a bit different too. In a restaurant several of us ordered steaks. When the waitress brought the cooked steaks to the table each steak had two fried eggs, sunny side up, on the top of the steaks. When we asked her how come, she said, "That's how we eat stiiik and iiiigs. Try it, you'll like it." We found out a large dance hall pavilion called Crown Victoria Ballroom was open every evening with a standing invitation to all U.S. soldiers to come meet the Australian girls and dance. We had no problem finding the dance pavilion. It was big, and it was on a sandy seashore. It played American big band music. Most of the couples dancing were Australian military men in short pants and their dates in long dresses. I thought short pants on the dance floor were odd, but that was their style. We were inside the pavilion watching the dancers.

I don't remember exactly how it happened. I thought somebody tapped me on the shoulder. When I turned and looked, a very pretty young girl standing next to me said, "My name in Myra Carr. Would you like to dance with me?" I was caught off guard for a second, maybe surprised, but soon I almost shouted, "I would love to." After our first dance I thought she would leave me, go mingle, and dance with someone else, but she didn't. She danced with me again and again. I found I did not want to let her go. She was 18 or 20 years old, and I thought she was beautiful. She was there with a group of other girls and a chaperone to entertain the U.S. soldiers. She lived with her parents. Her brother was in the military service, she hoped to be a medical technician and she wished I would go home with her, meet her parents and have tea with them. The dance ended at midnight. I wanted to take her home, but she had to go back with the girls and their chaperone. The next day Myra Carr and I met at the Melbourne Zoo. We spent the day together. We did not go to her home to have tea, but we made other plans. That night, before she left me to go

3. Australia

home, she asked me to promise her I would come back to Australia after the war. I was holding her kind of close as I kissed her goodbye. I knew I would never see Myra Carr again.

In the morning at roll call we saw trucks and busses parked at the far end of our row of tents. The orders were to "eat breakfast, pack your bags, shake the straw out of your hair and be ready to leave camp immediately." After a short bus ride, we were standing in formation at a very familiar ship dock like the one we landed at about a week before. The large ship the soldiers were boarding was the *Kingsholm*. When we boarded the ship, the crewmen directed us through stairways and passageways to a group of cabins. The passageways were narrow and the cabins were small. Four men to a cabin was the order we received. Two bunks on top of each other at each side of the cabin took up all of the room. The men's rooms and showers were at the end of the hallway. Apparently the *Kingsholm* was a passenger ship, an ocean liner. Our cabins had to be rated third class or lower, or maybe they were the ship's crew's quarters when the ship was in non-military operations.

After I dropped my barracks bag on a bunk in one of the cabins, I worked my way up to the outside deck again. Soldiers were still boarding the ship and when the last soldier left the dock the boarding plank was removed from the ship. There were no bands playing and no young girls waving flags. In the late afternoon our ship slowly pulled away from the dock and headed for the open sea. It looked as if we had company. Two other ships in the bay started to move in the same direction. The port city of Melbourne was disappearing from the horizon. The people that lived there were so friendly to the Americans and the American soldiers loved them. I thought, "I will never forget Australia."

That evening we ate in what must have been the passenger dining room. It was big and pretty well decorated. The tables were wooden benches and we had seats to sit on. Some of my buddies chose to sleep on deck. They asked me to join them, but I stayed in the cabin on my bunk. I could not sleep. I tried to count how many times my father crossed the Atlantic between the United States and Europe. I traveled with him twice. I remembered the luxury cabins and the dining and the excellent service. I think he always traveled business or first class. I wondered how he would rate the accommodations we had on the *Kingsholm*?

The *Kingsholm* was a big ship and it wasn't as crowded as the last ship we were on. The guys were more relaxed. We had cabins to sleep in, the men's rooms were more accessible, you could take a freshwater shower at any time, the chow lines were shorter, the food was pretty good and you sat down to eat. What else could you ask for? How much better could it be? We were not traveling alone. Apparently we were one in a convoy of three ships. There was a ship far on the horizon on the right side of our ship and another ship on our left side. They were almost fun to watch. The ocean was choppy and at times it looked as if the ships on the horizon dove into the waves never to come up again, but then they would surface. If you watched them long enough, you either became hypnotized or seasick from the effect. The ships were traveling northeast. They were zigzagging and within a day we knew where we were going: New Caledonia, an island occupied by the French about a thousand miles off the northeastern coast of Australia. In past centuries it was colonized by French political prisoners. It is a tropical island 300 miles long and about 50 miles wide; on the map it looks like a small worm. It took us eight days to get there. It was March 12, 1942.

4.

New Caledonia

We pulled into a large bay at the very southern tip of the island into the port town of Nouméa. The tip of the island surrounded the natural bay, excellent for warships and troop movement. It became our station of operations. In the bay and at the docks there were troop ships, freighters, aircraft carriers and a few U.S. Navy warships. One was pretty big. It had to be a cruiser. There was no small boat activity in the bay at all and from a distance the town looked deserted. U.S. military men seemed to have control of the docks. When our ship docked the first men off were the infantry and artillery companies or the combat troops. They were going to occupy the upper parts of the island to make sure the island would be secure.

While still on board we were informed the 22nd Ordnance Company would be stationed in the town of Nouméa. Our job would be to maintain all weapons for the troops coming in and going out of this island. Our trucks, parts trucks, machine shop trucks, weapons carriers and all equipment shipped from California preceded us here. We would take possession of all our equipment as soon as we disembarked. I could never forget the date we got off the ship and stepped foot on the island of New Caledonia. It was a holy day, the Feast of St. Joseph. It was my father's birthday, March 19, 1942. U.S. Military Police (M.P.s) were all over the place. Within an hour the quartermaster company in charge of the Port of Nouméa released to us 18 of our trucks and all our equipment, parked in a large waterfront warehouse. Everything we packed in the trucks in Camp Leonard Wood, Missouri, was there in good order. All of our men, the company commander, the officers and sergeants gathered in a group. It felt good. We were an ordnance company again.

All of our trucks started as if they were driven regularly. I got to drive my little truck, the weapons carrier I used to drive to the firing range back

17,500 troops land in Nouméa, New Caledonia, March 12, 1942.

in camp. In convoy form we drove out of the dock area into the streets of Nouméa. There were no people on the streets. The houses we drove by had their doors and windows closed. Captain Coyle, in the convoy's first vehicle, a command car, was following an open car occupied by two men flying a small French flag. As we drove by what looked like a police station, a few men in French military uniforms stood at attention and saluted us.

About a quarter of a mile past the military station, going up a hill, the lead car turned right on to a paved road. The very first building on the right side of the road was a beautiful, white mansion with a high flagpole with an American flag flying in the wind. A few hundred feet farther, the convoy stopped. We were at the end of the road overlooking the most beautiful view of the entire bay. On the right side just above the road an ancient French Legionnaires' garrison, a fort with high stone walls and a massive gate like you see in the movies, was majestically standing there ready to take on any foe coming into the bay. It was an excellent station for a cannon shot. Below the fort down to the bay, an area the size of a football field was pretty clear of brush, perhaps used by the fort for a parade ground.

4. New Caledonia

Captain Coyle and his lieutenants and sergeants were standing at the edge of the road talking to the two men from the lead car, pointing fingers at the field. Two of the officers and the first sergeant stepped off the road and started walking down towards the beach as if performing a land survey, pacing and motioning with their arms. Everybody was watching. Almost immediately Captain Coyle's command car drove off the road toward the men. The sergeants standing on the road motioned the convoy to follow. Slowly each truck left the road and followed the vehicle in front of it. When the last truck left the road and the convoy stopped, we were in a giant semi-circle about 300 feet in length, parallel to the beach. Looking up we saw the French fort, and looking down we saw the bay.

It took us two days to convert that field into a tent city with a command post, a mess hall, showers, latrines, and a parking lot. The pyramidal tents were up in no special order, four men to a tent. James Bertie, Ralph Clark, Tommy Mitchell and I put up our tent next to a path a two minute walk from the beach. Our maintenance guys screwed pieces of galvanized pipe together, made a flagpole, dug it into the ground next to the tent used as our command post, and with a little ceremony and a blast on a trumpet, we raised our flag. This was our camp. It became our home for the next seven months.

First Sergeant Van Meter told us the captain was very pleased with the way we put up our camp. The captain had a habit of passing out rewards for jobs well done. The rewards were time off, a weekend, one or two days or even an afternoon to do as we pleased. Captain Coyle was a tough guy but fair. Everybody liked him and I think he liked the guys. He knew the guys by name. He called me Alex K. because my name was too hard to pronounce for a Texan. The sergeant told us the captain gave the company the rest of the day off. We could go to Nouméa to tour the town if we wished. He said, "Go in pairs, carry no weapons, stay out of trouble and be back in camp by midnight."

After a record breaking shave, shower and shampoo, the guys started walking into town. Ralph Clark, Jim Bertie and I were not far behind. We had to walk by the French Legionnaires Fort and the white mansion with the flagpole with the American flag on it. We later found out the mansion was being prepared to be headquarters for U.S. Army general Patch. When we turned the corner and walked down the hill past what looked like a police station we were in town. This was about a 15 minute walk. The sidewalks were narrow, the houses were wooden, one floor structures built

General A. Patch's headquarters a few hundred feet from the French Army fort in Nouméa, New Caledonia, 1942.

next to each other. Within a block from the police station we walked into a good-sized square with a gazebo, flowers, and benches. It looked like the town's park. There were absolutely no people on the streets. All the houses had their doors and windows closed. The only life and movement we could see in town was U.S. Army trucks moving here and there. They were moving equipment and troops from the shipping docks. A couple of U.S. sailors asked us where they could buy some beer or wine or something to drink. We told them we were looking too. One of the areas looked like the town's marketplace, but the storefronts were boarded with shutters. This town was closed down tight. For a time it looked as if the people closed up their homes and left town.

We walked up to a very beautiful church. The sign on the wall read St. Joseph's Cathedral. The cathedral had two towers, two high stairways leading to a very nicely decorated entrance. Two elderly gentlemen were sitting on the steps smoking their pipes while we stood there looking up at the cathedral. The two gents tilted their hats at us in a friendly manner. We gave them a hand salute. We saw a few older people walking around the cathedral's courtyard. Two sailors walked out of the cathedral and

4. New Caledonia

walked down the stairway. When they reached the street level one of them said, "The church is open if you want to go in." I was a churchgoer, but Jim Bertie was a professed atheist. I don't know how we became friends. We didn't go in the church; we walked back to the center of town.

All of a sudden the town's mood changed. People began appearing, standing in doorways and looking out of windows. Some made friendly hand motions as we walked by. There were more sailors than soldiers walking the streets. We met a few sailors carrying bottles of wine. We asked them where they got the wine from. They pointed in a direction where a store was opened somewhere, but we could not find the place. On a street with large old trees and a much eroded sidewalk caused by tree roots, I caught my foot in a sidewalk crack, stumbled, but caught myself from falling by grabbing onto the corner of a nearby house. When I straightened out and looked up, I was looking down a narrow walkway between two houses. A young lady standing in a street level window was looking at me, and I thought she was laughing. She looked young and she was pretty. For a moment I just stood there looking at her. She didn't move. I started walking toward her and when I got close to her, she pulled the window shutters closed. I couldn't see any glass on the other side of the shutters. I could sense she was standing there.

My two buddies standing at the entrance to the walkway were watching me. With my fingers I tapped on the window shutter once, then tapped again and waited. Nothing. I was ready to leave when suddenly, with lightning speed, the shutters flew open and the girl shoved a bottle of wine into my chest. I grabbed the bottle and she pulled the shutters closed. She caught me so off guard that I didn't know what to say. I think I said, "Thank you. What do I owe you? I will pay you, mercie." There was no answer. Apparently the adventure ended. It was over. We walked down the street, opened the bottle and drank the wine. For some reason I wanted to go back to the window with the fast moving shutters. I think I wanted to pay the girl for the wine. That's what I thought I wanted to do.

While my two buddies were conversing with a couple of sailors, I slipped away and walked back to the walkway between the houses. In my hand I held a few dollar bills. I walked up to the window and with my fingers tapped on the shutters. There was no answer. Again, I tapped a little bit harder and waited. I heard a click, the shutters opened and the girl stood there looking at me, she was smiling. She was much prettier than I thought she was. I always was a pretty nervy young man, but if ever

I felt foolish it was when I picked up my hand with the dollar bills and said, "I want to pay you for the wine." She put up her hands and said, "No, no, no," in a very heavy French accent. She pointed her finger at me and said, "You name?" I said, "My name is Alex." She repeated my name several times dragging the letter x, it sounded like a very French name. I said, "What is your name?" She was looking at me and smiling she said in that French accent, "My name is Jean Pulier." The way she said it, it almost sounded like the beginning of a song. I said, "Jean Pulier, that's a very nice name." I didn't know how to carry on a conversation with her, but I didn't want to leave. I said, "Do you speak English?" She sort of waved her hand as if waving the subject off and rattled on an entire sentence in French. I didn't understand and then she said, "A little bit." In a little while, standing there I reached out and touched her hand. She didn't move. To keep things going, thinking she would understand short sentences, I said, "Nouméa is a nice town. New Caledonia is a beautiful island. Where are all the people?"

As time went by, soldiers and sailors walking by glanced my way wondering what I was doing at the window. It made me feel uneasy. I thought she felt the same way. Suddenly she stepped back, away from the window, and with her hand motioned to me to come. She said, "Alex, enter." The window sill was about waist high. I hesitated, looking at her, and again she motioned with her hand and said, "Alex, you come." When I told my buddies what happened next, they didn't believe me, but it was true. In a second, like an acrobat, I spanned the window sill. I was inside the room and she pulled the window shutters closed and locked the latch. When she turned, she was facing and standing right next to me. She did not move. I put my arms around her waist and kissed her. She kissed me back. Soon she backed away, took my hand and let me to another room. She pointed to a small table and a couple of chairs, said something in French, and then in a very French accent said, "Alex, sit."

She placed bread and cheese on the table and opened a bottle of wine. I ate some bread and a piece of cheese and drank the wine. She spoke to me in French and added a few words in English. I am sure she knew I didn't understand everything she said, but I thought she was getting something off her chest by talking to me. I did understand that she was married and had a four year old little girl. Her husband, a Vichy French military officer, was arrested and deported to Hebrides Island just before the Americans came. Her father, a school professor, lived in Nouméa and her brother

4. New Caledonia

owned a farm in nearby Dumbeia Valley. That's where the little girl was. Later that evening she told me she was 27 years old. I was almost 22. We drank some more wine. She told me she wasn't concerned for her husband because he wasn't good to her. He liked other women. She was speaking French and some English, but somehow I started to understand almost everything she was saying. It was getting dark and very warm. Standing there, somehow she turned and her dress fell from her body to the floor. I looked. That instant I thought she was gorgeous. I remember she helped me take off my shirt. Just before the evening ended, we were in an enclosed outdoor shower enjoying the cool water. In a million years I never dreamed I would find myself in a shower with a very pretty French girl on my very first leave in the town of Nouméa. Lucky for me I found my way back to camp just before midnight.

For the next few weeks company activities dominated everything else. Very near the shipping docks the company acquired a large warehouse with a big parking area for a repair shop. Clean up took a few days. Enough lumber was brought in from somewhere to build work tables, storage racks and benches. For awhile I thought I was a carpenter. My father taught me

22nd Ordnance bin truck with parts parked next to repair shop in Nouméa, New Caledonia.

to swing a heavy hammer. Lieutenant Ben Rabin, our Small Arms Section officer, helped us pick one side of the building for our repair department. The artillery repair and automotive sections took up the biggest part of the building. With some luck and good management by Captain Coyle and his staff of officers and sergeants, the 22nd Ordnance Company had a large repair shop and was ready for business. Every morning after breakfast we drove our trucks from our camp to the repair shop, about a 15 minute ride. We drove back to camp for lunch and repeated the same schedule for the afternoon work period. We drove back to camp at the end of the day.

As our army poured into New Caledonia through the port of Nouméa, immediately the army units were transported by truck to the upper part of the island which the French called the Bush. For the French, going to the upper part of the island was like going to another world. Army camps were constructed along the dirt highway for the entire length of the island, about 300 miles. Two large army trucks passing each other had a hard time. Some of the mountains were high and some of the ravines measured a thousand feet down or even more. New Caledonia, one of the world's greatest producers of nickel, used its processed nickel ore, dark orange in color, to surface the highway. Everything along the highway, trees and bushes from the dust had an orange glow. Drivers using the highway acquired the same orange glow.

Captain Coyle, received an order from the general's office that every weapon on the island, small arms and artillery, was to be inspected. Only weapons needing repair would come to the repair shops in Nouméa. All weapon inspections were to be performed in the field at their location by ordnance men. I think Sergeant Charles Mooney was the first one to tell me about the inspections. He said, "The captain is going to pick two teams to do the inspections, small arms and artillery. I think your name is on the small arms team. You know guns and you're a good driver." Charles Mooney was an old army man from the south. He taught me a lot about guns and how to play double deck pinochle. He had a little problem. He liked to booze it up. When we played cards, if I made a mistake, he called me "you big recruit." I liked him. The sergeant was right. I was in the first small arms inspection group and also the driver in charge of the bin truck. The bin truck was big. It looked like a school bus with windows all around, but it was very dependable with its four-wheel drive. The truck was equipped with workbenches and the necessary tools. Gun parts were stored

4. New Caledonia

in small drawers throughout the truck making it a real traveling workshop.

Our first field weapons inspection was a new experience for me. I thought it was for all of us. Staff Sergeant Roy Horsley, Lt. R.E Druba and their men led the way in a command truck. The rest of the crew followed with me driving the bin truck. An infantry regiment camped near Dumbeia Valley barely 12 miles along the dirt highway was not hard to find. We found their rifles, machine guns and handguns clean and in good condition. We field gauged maybe every third or fourth rifle, and that saved us time. We made some repairs. The regiment's commanding officer didn't think an inspection of his unit's weapons was necessary. He was not pleased. It seemed to me that the commander thought we were sent there to inspect something that did not need inspection.

It did not take us long to learn that nobody liked the word inspection. It somehow degraded the ones being inspected. We made the change. We became known as the traveling service and repair unit that checked all types of weapons and if need be repaired them. When we found our niche, we were welcome every place we went.

In the seven months we spent in New Caledonia I traveled the length of the island several times. Most of our service trips were but a few days, but the trips to the upper part of the island took as much as two weeks. The highway, the villages and all of the island's activities were on the west side of the island. The east side was jungle. Our officers lost the desire to travel the dirty, dusty highway. The repair men were rotated and later I even had my choice of men to take with me. I never got off the so-called inspecting team.

Every time I had a chance, at least once a week, I went to visit Jean. She was always very friendly and passionate and she always told me she was waiting for me. I believed her. She always had something tasty to eat and always had wine. The New Caledonia wine was rationed. She told me her ration of wine was 27 bottles a month as per all adults. I drank a lot of her wine and took some of it for my friends. On one occasion on a Sunday we drove to Dumbeia Valley to her brother's farm. I met her brother, Ermond, his wife, Tesa and Jean's father, the professor. He had a little mustache and a goatee; he looked like a professor. And there I met Jean's little daughter. Her name was Jeanine. She was small, she had dark hair and she was very pretty. Her brother and his wife had no children. I thought perhaps that's why little Jeanine was living there.

Jean's father spoke some English. He talked about the war, how he didn't like the Germans or the Japanese or the Vichy French, and I thought he didn't like Jean's husband.

While the professor did all the talking, Jean and Tesa set a table fit for a king. The dinner was a French banquet, the best I had since I left my mother's table. The professor told me the story about his great-great-great-grandfather who said something nasty about Napoleon. He was arrested, convicted, and deported to New Caledonia as a political prisoner. The professor had a meaningful desire to someday visit France; he had never been there.

When we got back to Nouméa to Jean's home, it was late. She wanted me to come in for a while, but I thought it was late. I had to get back to camp. She tempted me, shower and all. Women have a way with men, and Jean used well her God-given charm. What man can resist?

From our campsite and our in town shop we watched troop ships, cargo ships, and navy destroyers entering the Nouméa harbor. The dock areas were used day and night around the clock. Army trucks big and small filled the streets. There were no traffic signals. Driving or walking on the streets you were on your own.

The open stores were overrun by soldiers and sailors. Wine, the most sought after product, jumped from a few French francs to several dollars a bottle, if you could find it. A small hotel in town became a hangout for officers.

On the road leading out of town, near the nickel docks on a hillside were two government controlled bordellos, cathouses. The two large houses were next to each other. They were open 24 hours a day. To accommodate the vast business, it was known that the ladies working there were being imported from other islands. Some came from as far as Australia and New Zealand. Going out of town I traveled that road many, many times and observed the action on the famous hilltop. Soldiers and sailors stood in a long line waiting their turn at one of the lovely ladies. I was told the ladies were hand picked and the price was right. I thought, "Maybe someday, just to see the place and the girls we'll have to make a stop there."

Sometimes things turn out right, and sometimes they just don't.

It was early afternoon. Jim Bertie, Ralph Clark and I finished our service work at a small army unit stationed high in the mountains along the nickel ore covered road about fifty miles north of Nouméa.

The road was treacherous. Some inclines and declines were miles

4. New Caledonia

long. It was going to take us at least two hours driving time to get back to our camp. It was Ralph Clark who made the suggestion.

He said, "It's early. We have plenty time. Let's make a stop at the hilltop house across from the nickel dock. Let's check the place out."

I was a little bit surprised at what Ralph suggested. He was so reserved and quiet. I looked at Jim, but he didn't say anything. Ralph had a beautiful girlfriend back home. I saw her picture many times. She was a beauty from Indiana, but of course, Indiana was a long way from here.

We gathered our tools, loaded the workbench into the bin truck and cleaned up the work area.

When we were ready to leave Jim said, "Alex, let me drive the bin truck. If we make that stop Ralph mentioned, you'll need your rest."

Jim was a good driver. He drove the bin truck many times before on what some men called The Devil's Highway.

When we got to the main road, Jim turned the truck south. I settled in the front seat and Ralph got comfortable in the extra seat right behind me. There was some traffic on the road, all U.S. Army vehicles, trucks, command cars, and jeeps. A safe travel speed was 20 to 25 miles per hour and in some places along the road you had to bring your speed down to a crawling pace. It was well known that some speed demon drivers with no brains drove their vehicles off the road into thousand foot ravines, never to be heard from again.

We were about halfway to Nouméa at a high spot in the mountains when Jim double-clutched the truck and shifted into a lower gear to start the drive down a very long decline. The truck had four forward gears plus overdrive. To keep the truck moving at a safe pace, you had to shift from gear to gear going up a hill to get to the top. You also had to shift the gears down to slow the truck down when going down the hill. In my opinion, the truck was moving down the hill a little too fast. Jim was pumping the brake pedal.

In a loud voice I said, "Jim! You're going too fast!"

Jim hollered back, "The truck has no brakes!"

Ralph grabbed my shoulder from the back seat and he and I almost with one voice hollered, "Gear the truck down!"

The truck was moving about 25 miles per hour. Down to the bottom of the hill was about a mile or more. Jim had his eyes glued to the road. He kept pumping the brake pedal down and pulling and releasing the hand brake.

585 Raids and Counting

Almost in a commanding voice I said, "Jim, gear the truck down."

Jim hollered back, "Okay, okay, okay! I will, I will!"

Jim double clutched the transmission and threw the gear shift into a lower gear. We could feel a forced slow down surge. Jim shifted down to another gear, and the truck slowed down to half its original speed. Luckily for us, there were no trucks coming up or going down the hill. Jim shifted one more time into the truck's lowest gear.

By the time we got to the bottom of the hill in its low gear and Jim's hand on the hand brake, the truck was under Jim's command. He stopped the truck on the outside of the road. We looked under the truck but couldn't see or find anything broken. We were about 25 miles from our camp and we had to get there somehow.

After a pee call, Jim said, "Alex, it's your truck. You drive!"

To Jim, Ralph in his sheepish way said, "I think you earned some kind of medal for bringing that truck down the hill in one piece. I'll make you one."

I drove. As we got closer to Nouméa, traffic increased and I had to keep the truck in its lowest gear. Frustrated drivers behind us were tooting their horns. I tried to keep to one side of the road to let the smaller vehicles pass us.

It was dark and late when we drove by the nickel docks and the two famous houses on the hilltop. A group of sailors were walking toward town.

I stuck my arm out, waved, and shouted, "How long are the lines?"

One of the guys shouted back, "Not long, half hour waiting time."

I glanced at Jim in the passenger seat. He was sound asleep.

"Ralph, you awake?" I asked. There was no answer.

When I pulled into our camp it was midnight. I said, "When we drove by the nickel docks, you guys were asleep. I tried to wake you up. The lines were short."

Ralph said, "Maybe next time. There's always next time."

For me next time never came.

After every inspection trip I had to report to Lieutenant Ben Rabin and give him a pretty thorough account on all we did. What regiment or company did we see, how did we do, what parts did we use and did we keep count, did we finish the job and did we have any problems?

Lieutenant Rabin was my favorite officer. He treated me like a younger brother. I thought he gave me more credit for knowing guns and doing my job than I deserved. He told me a request had been made by the gen-

4. New Caledonia

French soldiers watching gate to French Army fort in Nouméa, New Caledonia.

eral's office to show and teach the French military how to use U.S. Army small arms weapons. He thought, perhaps, U.S. Army weapons would be issued to the French Army garrison.

He said, "As soon as a date and place is set I want you to be one of the crew, one of the instructors. We'll take Leo Langlas with us; he'll help us with the French."

Private Leo Langlas was of French descent. He came from Massachusetts, and he spoke French as well as any Frenchman. When in need the company used Leo as an interpreter. The date came up very fast and the place was the French Army fort right above our camp.

We loaded two trucks with rifles, pistols, .30 and .50 caliber machine guns, and tripods and drove up to the fort's gates. The fort's stone walls were about 20 feet high and several feet thick. The top of the wall was covered with shattered glass bottles, very hard for an enemy to climb across.

The guards opened the iron gates and showed us where to park our trucks. It took us about a half hour to set up our weapons display. We had rifles and pistols placed on folding tables and machine guns on tripods as if ready for action. Everything was easy to see or touch.

A few French soldiers were walking around the grounds and some were standing in the doorways of the building that looked like their living quarters. A French sergeant walked up to us and in English asked us if we were ready. When we told him yes he walked back to the building. We waited and waited and waited. Finally, after about an hour's wait, six French officers walked out of the building and came our way. They were in a group and they were laughing about something. Two native black soldiers in short pants and big shoes walked behind the officers about 10 feet away. The top ranking officer, a colonel, was surrounded by the other officers as if being protected from something. He was smoking a long cigarette. For a moment I visualized Jean's husband. If he was still here would he have fit in to this picture?

When the French officers approached our display, Lieutenant Rabin saluted the colonel. The French officers returned the salute. I heard the colonel say something to Lieutenant Rabin. I thought it was a greeting. The officers spent very little time looking at the weapons. They just walked by. They were more interested in the handguns, the pistols, than anything else.

As soon as the officers walked away from our display, a dozen native black soldiers gathered around our guns. They picked up the rifles, touched

4. New Caledonia

Alex Kunevicius and French soldier, Nouméa, New Caledonia, 1942.

the machine guns, and checked the handguns, but nothing was asked and nothing was said. If I had had to write a report on this meeting, I wouldn't have known what to say.

The officers standing a few feet away in a circle must have been telling jokes because they were laughing at something. The colonel had to be a chain smoker because every time he put a cigarette in his mouth, every other officer stuck a lighter under his nose.

After several hours of just standing around, the officers went into the building and something very unexpected happened. A soldier came out of the building, came up to us, said something in French and motioned for us to follow him. Good thing we had Leo Langlas with us. He said, "We are invited to have lunch with the officers. Follow the soldier."

The inside of the building looked like a fortress with thick walls, concrete floors, and small windows. When the soldier led us into the dining room, the officers were sitting at a long table drinking wine. Large pieces of cut bread, tropical fruit and wine glasses covered the table. As soon as we sat down a soldier poured red wine out of a pitcher into everybody's wine glasses. Two girls started serving soup, fish, small pieces of meat and something that looked like cooked grass. The two girls did some of the serving and a lot of flirting with the officers. Both girls were dark skinned, young and very pretty. The officers paid more attention to the one named René. She seemed to be their favorite.

When we drove out of the fort that afternoon, I thought every one of us felt somewhat foolish; maybe that's what the French officers were laughing about — "To them, we were the joke!"

Our guys who participated in that infamous French fort venture had but one question: "What was that cooked grass we were eating?" It was good. When I told Jean what happened to us at the fort with the French officers she wasn't surprised. She told me the French officers were good at two things only. They liked to drink wine and loved to play with beautiful girls. She said her husband was a member of that group. She knew the girl named René. She was beautiful but no good. Jean thought her husband had something to do with her. She lived near the nickel docks, a very dangerous place. The bordellos were there and places where sailors went to meet girls and get drunk.

Jean, talking about her husband, René, and the nickel docks worked herself into a slight frenzy. She pointed and shook her finger at me and said, "Alex, you no go nickel docks. No, no, no!"

4. New Caledonia

I didn't have the heart to tell her I was there.

It was either May or June when dark clouds hung over the bay. The rains came and the wind was fierce. The word was out a hurricane was coming.

Most of the guys in our company never experienced a hurricane or even heard of one. I never lived through anything more than a cool Ohio breeze.

The French fort colonel must have had a heart. He offered our company commander a place to gather the company behind the fort's walls during the storm, but our company commander refused the offer. We thought Captain Coyle, a Texan, knew something about hurricanes. He gave the orders.

The first order was to tie down the tents and secure your gear. We placed heavy rifle boxes inside the bottom of the tent flaps and tied them down. Everything in the tent was picked up off the ground and stacked on the folding cots. Before our mess hall two-pole tent was brought down on top of all the cooking gear and tied down. The company cooks opened cans of Spam, sliced them in big pieces and handed them to the men. That was our rations during the storm.

A detail of men drove to town to secure our workshop. They stayed there. All of the Nouméa houses were equipped with window shutters. They were closed, and there was nobody on the streets. The people of this island knew how to handle a hurricane. We didn't.

A second order came from the company commander. Drive our trucks in between our tents from the bayside where possible, and anchor the tents to the trucks.

Jim Bertie and I managed to bring the bin truck to our tent area and we did the best we could with the rope we had. Some of the guys were not so lucky. Some of the trucks got stuck in the soft wet ground. Toward the late afternoon and evening, the wind and rain was so severe you couldn't hear yourself think. The four of us couldn't hear each other talk. We were wet and it was cold, and the tent was flapping in all directions. At times, the tent lifted and expanded like a big balloon. The ropes held, but the wooden pegs holding the ropes were pulled out of the wet ground.

During the night, water started flowing through the tent and the tent collapsed. Somehow I was caught leaning over a gun case with my knees in the water and the canvas tent flapping on top of me. It had to be the worst time of the storm when I heard one of the guys scream, "Let's get out of here! Let's get in the truck!"

585 Raids and Counting

I don't know why we didn't think of that before. It was pitch black. I couldn't see. On my hands and knees I crawled until I found my way out from beneath the canvas tent. The four of us got out, found the door to the truck, got in and collapsed.

When morning came, the rain was still coming down, but the wind had died down. The worst of the storm was over. We got out of the truck and looked around. The camp was devastated. All of the tents were on the ground, none were standing. Some of the guys were walking around as if lost, and some were trying to pick up their tents again. The tents were not really damaged. The ropes held. It was the pegs pulled out of the sopping wet ground and the ballooning effect that lifted the tents off of the tent pole fasteners. The tent poles slipped through the air vents and the tents came down.

Almost everybody had the same story of how and why their tents came down. Maybe we learned a lesson how to keep our tents up during a wind storm. In a day or two, the camp was up and the 22nd Ordnance Company was back in business.

My French speaking buddy Leo Langlas asked me if I would do him a favor. He was in my small arms section and I often took him on inspection trips with me.

I said, "Sure, Leo, what do you need?" Leo told me about a family in town he made friends with. The man, Pierre, a professional fisherman, had a motorized boat. He caught fish and lobsters to make a living. He had a problem. His gasoline ration was small. He could use a few gallons of gas.

I liked Leo. This was not exactly what I liked to do, but when a guy needs a favor, do him a favor. I had access to two of our vehicles; the bin truck and a weapons carrier, a small pickup truck. Each army truck carried extra gas, a five gallon tank secured to each side of the truck's running board. One evening, Leo and I took a ride to the place his friend Pierre kept his fishing boat. I met Pierre, a nice man. We emptied our two five gallon tanks into a gas drum. Pierre thanked us and we drove back to camp. I thought someday I'll confess my sin to a priest, my penance should not be heavy. After all, I did a man a favor. The good Lord will understand that.

A few days later Leo told me we were invited to Pierre's house for a lobster dinner. Pierre said grace, and the dinner was fantastic. Pierre's wife, Louisa, outdid herself. His wife, two little girls, and a boy sat at one side

4. New Caledonia

of the table. I was seated next to Pierre's father, an older gentleman that kept pouring champagne into my glass. Leo sat next to Pierre and translated the fishing stories Pierre kept telling, but I thought the best story of the night was told by Pierre's wife, Louisa.

She said, "When Pierre comes home after a fishing trip, he first goes to see his lady friend, Fefie, then he comes home." Then she added, "Of course that way I get my rest."

Pierre laughed. His father laughed so hard, he swung his arm and knocked my glass of champagne over onto my lap.

Instantly, Pierre, his wife, and father jumped out of their chairs, pointed their fingers at me and kept shouting something with large smiles on their faces.

Leo tried to tell me what was going on but was overwhelmed with the family's joyous action. When the family settled down, Leo explained that I was a very lucky man. To have someone spill champagne on you by accident was the greatest luck omen in the world. I was and would be extremely lucky. The evening ended on that note. I thanked Pierre and his wife for a lavish dinner and a very nice evening and went back to camp with wet pants.

5.

St. Joseph's Cathedral

Unless you were on some special detail, Sundays were pretty much a day when you could do as you please. It was a good day to write letters home, do your laundry, go swimming in the bay, go to town or just sleep.

Every Sunday morning, a group of Catholic guys went to Nouméa St. Joseph Cathedral for Mass. I always went and tried to get my tentmates to go with me. Ralph Clark, from Winamac, Indiana, was a Methodist; Tommy Mitchell, from Flint, Michigan, was a Lebanese Orthodox Christian; and my best buddy, Jimmy Bertie, from Pittsburgh, Pennsylvania, was an atheist. Maybe that's why they didn't go, but they always urged me to go pray for myself and for them too.

Joe Bargiel, Eddy Drozdz, and Frank Gornik, all from Cleveland, Ohio, always went so I had company. We had permission to drive a small truck so we didn't have to walk, even though it was only about a 15 minute walk from camp to the cathedral.

The local people attending Mass at the cathedral made the soldiers and sailors feel welcome. Sometimes the French priest saying the sermon would slip in a few words in English just to let us know that he knew that we were there.

Many times after Mass in the courtyard, I had seen local women hand a solder or sailor a sweet croissant or some tasty morsel, perhaps, to show them their motherly love.

This particular Sunday, the cathedral had a large number of visiting U.S. sailors, all in white uniforms. This was a very special Sunday for all the soldiers and sailors. It was the week of the 4th of July 1942.

After the sermon, the priest in English wished the soldiers and sailors a happy 4th of July, and then added, "It was the French who helped George Washington achieve his goal."

After Mass at one side of the courtyard, a group of local women were

5. St. Joseph's Cathedral

St. Joseph's Cathedral Nouméa, New Caledonia. U.S. Army and Navy men attended Mass there, 1942.

standing around several tables packed with bread and cheese and something that looked like crackers with pieces of fruit on top. A man was slicing the bread and cheese. Several little boys and girls standing among the women were waving small American flags.

The women encouraged the soldiers and sailors to help themselves to the morsels. I thought this was a beautiful gesture the French ladies displayed, celebrating one of our beloved holidays.

We helped ourselves to the bread and cheese and exchanged questions and answers with the sailors. The sailors asked and we gave answers the best we could to the best places to buy a bottle of wine. We were the old timers on the island.

Most conversations started with where are you from, how long have you been on this rock, or what ship are you from? Sometimes, just meeting someone from your home state made your day a little better.

The crowd was thinning out. We were at our truck climbing in when a navy petty officer ran up to us and with some anxiety told us he had an injured sailor at the bottom of the stairs leading to the street. He fell, and he couldn't walk. The petty officer wanted to know if we would drive him to the first aid station.

One of our guys said, "Jump in."

We drove the truck to the street and stopped at the front of the concrete stairway. A sailor was lying on the ground, not moving. Another sailor kneeling on one knee was holding a cloth around the injured man's head. A group of sailors was standing around watching.

Immediately, by the petty officer's request, sailors picked up the injured man and gently laid him down in the truck. It took our driver less than ten minutes to get the sailor to the nearby first aid station.

At the station a corpsman first checked the injured sailor, then they put him on a stretcher and carried him inside. The petty officer went in with them.

We waited maybe for ten or fifteen minutes to see if the sailor was going to be all right. The petty officer came out and told us the sailor would be fine. The young man knocked himself out falling down those concrete steps. He'd have to be more careful if he ever got to be at St. Joseph's Cathedral again. He thanked us for our help and started walking away. Suddenly the petty officer turned and wanted to know if any of us were ever on an aircraft carrier or on any navy fighting ship.

All of us had the same answer. "No."

5. St. Joseph's Cathedral

He asked us if we would like to go on one as his guest, have lunch on board, and then he would show us around the ship.

Joe Bargiel and Frank Gornik were the first to say yes.

It was Sunday. We had all day. I decided I'd go.

The three of us got out of the truck. Some of the guys hemmed and hawed and decided to go back to camp. The petty officer told us his name was John Kall. He was from the state of Missouri, and now he was serving duty on the navy carrier.

He said, "We'll be here for a few days for a short rest period. Wait a few minutes. Let me make sure they get that sailor to the right ship when they release him," and he walked back into the first aid station. When he came out he told us the sailor was going to be fine and said, "Let's go to the pier."

Because it was Sunday, several landing craft were transporting sailors from ship to shore and shore to ship, making it easy for the sailors to spend some time on shore visiting the port city of Nouméa.

We boarded one of the landing craft and within a very short time we climbed up a ramp of a large aircraft carrier. We got off the ramp at an opening at a lower deck then walked up some stairs to an open deck. We were at the center of the ship at the large command structure. When we got to the corner of the structure we could see the front and rear end of the ship. The deck looked like a mile long. There were two planes parked at one side of the runway. A few men were doing something to the planes. Kall told us the planes were stored in a large area below the main deck. During operations, a large elevator brought the planes up to the main deck and only pilots and men working on the planes were allowed there. I believe he told us the runway was about a thousand feet long. It was long for sure. I couldn't believe my own eyes. I never saw anything like it. On both sides of the runway at a slightly lower level were rows of antiaircraft guns.

He explained that during operations when the planes were taking off or landing the noise and wind on deck was so strong the men working there had to wear protective gear for their eyes and ears, and even certain shoes to keep them from slipping off the runway.

He said, "Men working the runway during flight operations are very highly trained and dedicated. It's a very hard and dangerous job."

We had lunch in the galley, but the galley was not crowded. Since it was Sunday, the sailors got time off and most were eating in Nouméa.

After lunch, the petty officer walked us through a sizable area he called "the room of relaxation" for sailors while off duty, a place that looked like an army PX where you could buy cigarettes, shaving blades, and other needs. At the exit ramp Petty Officer John Kall thanked us again for helping his hurt sailor. We thanked him for the tour of the ship, got into the next Higgins boat and went to shore.

While going back to our camp, sitting in the back of the truck, the guys were quiet. I thought to myself this was a very nice Sunday. This morning we attended Holy Mass at a very beautiful St. Joseph's Cathedral. It was the 4th of July week, our most cherished freedom holiday. The French women and children celebrated, sort of, with their generosity, and we helped our neighbor in need. This was a very nice Sunday.

This was my third trip to the very northern end of the island. Almost all of our inspection trips were performed by six men. A two seat command car type truck with four guys led the way, and I drove the bin truck with a guy in the passenger seat.

As time went by and more and more troops were being settled along the dirt highway, army trucks carrying troops where everywhere. Every place and everything north of the town of Nouméa was called The Bush by the French people.

About 50 miles north of Nouméa at a place called Plentigalk, army engineers and a navy construction battalion were building an airfield. Most of the drivers driving the army dump trucks were from an army black regiment.

Because it was always hot, the drivers kept the truck windows opened. The orange dust from the nickel slag they were using to build the airfield runway colored them orange. Some of the local native workers with very large hairdos were interesting to see. They were black with orange hairdos glowing around their heads.

Traveling at 35 miles per hour on this narrow, slag-filled, dusty highway, sometimes you were taking your life into your hands if you were speeding. Climbing mile high hills and then going down again was pretty tricky. You had to double clutch the truck going all the way up the hill and you had to do the same going all the way down. Some of the inexperienced or car-less drivers missed the turns in the road and went off the road maybe, a thousand feet down into the jungle. Sometimes the drivers were badly hurt and the trucks never retrieved.

We were at the northern part of the island and for some reason we

5. St. Joseph's Cathedral

couldn't find the regiment's camp we were looking for. Most of the time, regiments or companies had signs posted along the road easy to see, but not this time. We drove all day, and we were tired and hungry. As a rule, we didn't carry any food with us because we always got to eat with the company whose guns we were inspecting.

"Take the second road to the right," a group of soldiers told us. They were sure the regiment we were looking for was down that road. We found the second road, there was no sign, but the commander car turned right and I slowly followed driving the bin truck.

Most of the side roads were very narrow, and sometimes the tree's branches were hanging over the road. It made it hard for a big truck to get through, and unless you found a place to turn around, you were stuck.

This road was narrow. It was all rock and instantly led down into a ravine. At the bottom of the ravine the road crossed a creek. The creek was about ten feet wide and a foot deep. It was rock bottom. The command car crossed the creek and I followed and crossed with no problem. The road went into a high incline then curbed around a large embankment and almost instantly we drove onto a large rocky plateau and there we saw what must have been the most beautiful part of the island. At our side of the rocky plateau, about 30 feet high, a waterfall was cascading down into a large rock created pool. Then the water overflowed the pool down the rocky hill most likely forming the creek we just crossed.

We stopped and got out of our trucks. There were children and native women near the waterfall. Some of the children were playing in the pool. In a short distance there were some small shacks and an old structure that looked like a western cowboy saloon.

We walked around the waterfall, admiring the beauty. All of us wondered why this place wasn't talked about by the French people in Nouméa, or proclaimed to be some sort of national park, and did it have a name?

We didn't have to wait long. A man was coming our way. He no doubt would tell us. He was an older man, well tanned with a mustache and goatee. He bowed to us in a friendly manner and greeted us in French, and then in English he said, "Good day." He told us very few people know about this place because it's so far from Nouméa. This place belonged to him and his family and he didn't mention a name.

He told us he spent several years in Australia working in the fish industry, but now he fished only to keep food on the table for his wives and children. His name was Phillipe. When we asked him if there were any army camps down the road he told us the road ended right there.

It was late afternoon, and it started to get dark. We thanked the man for his hospitality. We turned the trucks around and we were going to go back to the main road when something strange happened to us.

I think it started when the man asked us if we could spare him a few bullets for his .40 caliber revolver and if we would stay a little bit longer, his wives would prepare a tasty fish dinner for all of us. His wives would be honored if we would. We stayed.

I remember sitting at a large rounded table having a glass of wine and eating fish, bread, and some sort of vegetables. A kerosene lamp lit up the place. It was a little bit odd the man was not at the table. One of his wives brought in a good size platter filled with black shredded meat and placed it on the table. The meat was chewy but very tasty, and all of us had more than one helping. One of our own guys asked, "What is this stuff we're eating?" We heard a voice, like out of a cloud in very clear English say, "You are eating giant bat."

When I woke up it was morning. I was lying in a rickety bed with my clothes on, in a shack with no walls. Outside the shack I could see a native woman cooking something in a skillet on a charcoal fire. When I sat up she handed me a dish with something that looked like cooked spinach mixed with scrambled eggs. I ate a little bit, put the plate down, stepped out of the shack and walked to the trucks. All of us gathered there. Everyone looked puzzled. It was like a bad dream. Every one of us heard the voice saying, "You are eating giant bat," but after that, everything went blank for all of us. Was there something in the wine or was that meat drugged with some crazy potion? Why was it done, and what was the reason? All of us checked our pockets, everything was in order. The trucks were not touched, the doors were locked, we had the keys.

Some children and a few women were playing around the waterfall pool. One of our guys went over and asked the women, "Where is Mr. Phillipe?" The women shook their heads as if they never heard that name before.

We drove the trucks out of there, down the narrow road across the creek and up to the main road. About a mile down the highway we found a road with a large sign with an arrow pointing the way to the regiment we were looking for. On the way back to our camp, the six of us decided to say very little about the waterfall and the man named Phillipe. We didn't

5. St. Joseph's Cathedral

want our company commander to find out and ask us questions about our fantasy trip.

At times I asked myself was there really a man named Phillipe at the waterfall and was there a waterfall at the end of the second road we traveled on? Sometime later I asked Jean Paulier if she knew of any waterfall at the northern end of the island. She said, "I never heard of one."

Troop movements on the island intensified. My trips to the bush were shorter runs but many. Our in town shop became extremely busy receiving new weapons from the states and issuing them to the troops on the island.

The new M1 semi-automatic rifles started coming in in small numbers, and every unit wanted them. Every company commander wanted his men to have the new weapons, and some commanders went out of their way to get it done one way or another.

It was at our workshop in Nouméa a command car pulled into the yard occupied by some high ranking officers, two colonels and a major. The driver was a sergeant. Our Lieutenant Druba walked up to the group and gave them a hand salute. After a very short conversation with the officers, Lt. Druba went into the shop.

I was working on some handguns when Sergeant Horsley, a gun expert, came to me and said, "Alex, get your '03 rifle field gauges and come with me. We're going to look at some rifles."

Lt. Druba, Sgt. Horsley, and I in a small truck followed the officers' command car to a waterfront warehouse. Inside the warehouse, along one wall I saw '03 Springfield rifles stacked.

One of the colonels seemed very upset about something. I thought it was the way the rifles were stacked. I never saw rifles stacked that way before. Looking at us the colonel said, "I want your men to inspect these rifles. I want you to look at the rifles' bore, the rifling, and field gauge of each rifle. The serviceable rifles stand at the wall and the unserviceable put over there."

I was used to inspecting rifles as that was my job, but I never had two colonels and a major and a lieutenant watching me. With good care, the Springfield '03 rifle was a very serviceable, long lasting weapon unless damaged in battle or accident.

To claim a rifle unserviceable during a field inspection, other than some minor repairs, you had to find the rifle barrel pitted across both spiral grooves within the gun barrel or fail the rifle's bolts, the "go, or no go" gauge test. The 1903 Springfield rifle is 42 inches long, has a 20 inch

63

barrel, has a fine .30 caliber bullet holding chamber and weighs about 9 pounds. Sergeant Horsley and I started field testing the rifles. Every rifle we looked at proved to be in good condition. We stood them at the wall as good. We checked about 30 rifles at the first pile when Lt. Druba said, "Colonel Jacobson wants you to check a few rifles out of each pile. Start now." The sergeant and I walked from pile to pile checking the rifles and standing them at the wall. Out of about a hundred rifles checked we found no unserviceable rifles. The colonel told us to stop.

He said, "Sergeant, did you find any rifles unserviceable in the rifles you checked?"

"No, sir." The sergeant answered.

He said, "Young man, what's your name?"

I said, "Alex Kunevicius, sir."

Looking at me and the sergeant, the colonel said, "Good work, thank you."

Lieutenant Druba indicated this operation was over. We got into our truck and drove back to the shop. About a week later, Sergeant Horsley asked me if I wanted to know whey we were checking the rifles at the warehouse. He told me some high ranking officer took it upon himself to condemn all those rifles as unserviceable as a favor to some regiment commander who wanted the new M1 rifles for his men. That information somehow got to a higher officer who questioned the validity of that action. That's how the ordnance colonel, Jacobson, got involved. It was his call.

I never knew we had an ordnance colonel, but if so, Colonel Jacobson seemed to be a nice guy.

Sergeant Horsley said, "Those rifles came from some of the companies up in the bush. You probably looked at them before."

I thought I probably did.

6.

Company on the Move

It was late October 1942. Rumors spread throughout the company we were going to go to the Solomon Islands to help the Marines secure Guadalcanal.

A weekly newsletter issued by army headquarters gave very little information about any ground military action against the Japanese. We knew the Marines were fighting on Guadalcanal. Joe's odds were as good as any that's where we're going. Very soon the company was alerted to pack its gear and move to a holding area, a place called Dumbia Valley, 12 miles north of Nouméa along the dirt highway. I knew this area very well. I checked many soldiers' guns there for companies before they moved out.

It didn't take us long to set up camp. We were a small company of 120 men, but almost every man was a technician in some strategic field. Artillery, small arms, and field instruments were our expertise. We even had a watchmaker to fix soldiers' watches, Ernie Troski from Toronto, Ohio.

After a few days in our new camp, the guys were ready to move on. Waiting for something to happen was boring. Playing cards was the only game in camp. Eating Spam cold, hot, fried, sliced, or rolled in hot dog form, it was still Spam. We knew there were deer on the island. Our guys from down south, the hunters, decided to go hunting, possibly try to change our daily menu. Because I was a pretty good shot with a rifle, they took me with them, but I never hunted in my life. This was three real hunters and me. Sergeant Charlie Mooney took command. He knew where to go. We drove deep into a valley, to a creek; there were many trees and some farmland. After parking our truck we spread out and walked upward on both sides of the creek. I was told to walk at the lowest level of the creek's path. All of us walked in the same direction, only at different levels of the valley.

As I walked along the creek, the brush got thicker, and there were more trees. I stumbled over some rocks, and I couldn't see my hunting partners. I didn't think this was a good position to be in, and I didn't like hunting.

As we advanced, several times I heard Sergeant Mooney shout, "Anybody see anything?" And then it started. I heard a rifle shot and someone hollered, "I got one!" Then another shot. Someone hollered, "I got one." Then another shot. Someone hollered, "The deer is running up the creek, get him!" I looked. In the creek a large buck on his two front legs was dragging his hind two legs in the water with his head high in the air. The deer was badly hurt. It looked like the shooter hit the deer in the rear end, but the deer kept moving.

Sergeant Mooney shouted, "Alex, shoot the deer! Alex, shoot!" Apparently I was in the best position to shoot at the injured deer. I knelt down on one knee, took aim at the deer's head, and fired. The deer's head hit the ground instantly.

We gathered around the deer, he was big and had a nice rack. My good hunter friends gutted the buck and we pulled him into the truck. Going back to camp, I felt sorry for that beautiful buck, and promised myself I would never hunt again. That evening, the company had venison for supper. I had some. It was good.

Marlin Richards, our company clerk, and Joe Bargiel were pretty good friends. Joe and I were pretty good friends also. I always suspected Joe was getting some of his information about the company's upcoming activities from Marlin.

Joe had a good one this time. He told us a small group of men already picked, maybe twenty or so, would be first to leave for Guadalcanal as the front echelon. The company would follow a little bit later. The rumor spread fast throughout the company. When everyone in camp accepted the rumors as fact, our would-be war strategists came up with the reason why only a small number of men were going first.

They reasoned that this was going to be a large army infantry task force going to Guadalcanal to help the Marines fight the Japanese. There was not enough room on the invading ships to take all of us and our heavy equipment and trucks. Our advanced men would find a strategic location on Guadalcanal for the company to set up shop when it came. And then we had the company crepe hangers. Their version was this would be a trial run. The generals didn't want to risk losing the entire company and its

6. Company on the Move

heavy equipment. If the twenty men made it okay, the company would follow, and if not, well....

It was either the first, second, or third of November 1942. I'm not sure. The company was called out for roll call. First Sergeant Van Meter did the best he could to get the guys in some kind of formation, but standing at attention in the bush was hard to do.

Captain Coyle and his lieutenants approached the formation and bid it "at ease." The captain said, "The 22nd Ordnance Company is alerted to be ready to be transported to a combat zone, somewhere in the Solomon Islands. A cadre of two officers and twenty men will be first to leave at a moment's notice. The first men to leave.... Sergeant Van Meter, read the list."

The sergeant started with, "Lieutenant Benjamin Rabin, Sergeant Lawrence Deboni, Joseph Bargiel, James Bertie, Arthur Boessneck, John Burton, Ralph Clark, Lawrence Cox, Sid Garret, Frank Cornik, Edward Grody, Edward Kost, Alex Kunevicius, Merle McGawen, John McGrigan, Elmer Pluth, Peter Scazny, Conrad Tennent, Edgar Powell, Felix Stawicki, Francis VanBargen."

The sergeant stopped reading the list. It was very quiet. I heard my name called loud and clear and I swallowed hard. I think everyone on the list did. One good thing about the names on the list for me was my buddies James Bertie and Joe Bargiel, and Ralph Clark, and Art Boessneck, and Sid Garret were on the list too, and I liked Lieutenant Ben Rabin. He was a good, down to earth company officer.

The sergeant told the men whose names were on the list to stand still, and dismissed the rest of the company. Captain Coyle motioned to the standing men to get closer to him in a group. He told us, "The combat units on Guadalcanal were begging for ordnance men to handle the broken weapons. You men were picked to go there first because you're good at what you do. The entire company will follow as soon as the navy provides transport and landing ability for our heavy equipment and trucks."

The captain became very serious. He said, "Lieutenant Rabin will be with you men, and I wish you well," and he stepped back.

The sergeant told us we might be leaving tomorrow, or the next day or as soon as they got the notice. He told us to leave our excess clothing and personal things with the supply sergeant, that he would take care of things and would issue each of us a backpack. He said, "Go and pack now. Take a change of underclothes, your shaving stuff, your mess kit, and pack it in your backpack. Take your canteen, your helmet and your rifle, and get some sleep." Before the sergeant walked away, he said, "Don't forget to pack your tool kits. You'll need them."

The rest of the day was quiet. The men on the leaving list did their packing. It was the first week in November 1942.

Somehow the conversation in camp turned to how much combat training we had. Most of the men in this company, like me, were drafted and had no combat training at all. My basic training in Fort Knox, Kentucky, was six weeks of marching in formation on a large drill field with a loud sergeant, and firing a rifle at a target on the firing range. I probably had more rifle firing experience than most of the guys because at Fort Leonard Wood, Missouri, I was assigned to work on the firing range.

As I recall, none of the men scheduled to leave showed any kind of emotion about going into a combat zone. This was a job we had to do, I thought, and I was glad my closest friends were going with me. Maybe we were really not afraid or didn't want to show it, or we were just stupid, but that's the way it was.

I slept well that night until someone pulled my arm and said, "Get up, get your gear and fall out. We are leaving." It was dark. Someone lit a flashlight. Ralph Clark and Jim Bertie were also awake. It was 3:15 A.M. Within a half hour, the twenty men and two officers riding in two trucks were heading down the dirt highway towards Nouméa Harbor. We got out of our camp so fast and quietly, I didn't think the rest of the guys heard us go. In the morning they'd be surprised to see us gone.

When we drove into town, I thought of Jean. Since the company was alerted and went to Dumbia Valley, I never had a chance to see her again or tell her I was leaving New Caledonia. She might have thought I found someone I liked better than her. I'd probably never have an opportunity to tell her that wasn't so.

I knew Nouméa Harbor never closed. Workers and sailors worked it around the clock. It was still dark when we got there, but the pier was lit up very well, and it was full of activity. Apparently, troops were on the move. A very large number of soldiers in full combat gear were lined up on the pier waiting their turn to get into a landing craft to be transported to their assigned ships. The ships in bay with their lights on glowing against the water made a beautiful picture.

At least ten or more LCPs (Landing Craft Personnel) were carrying troops from the pier to the ships. More trucks arrived and more troops

6. Company on the Move

filled the pier. There was some shouting, sergeants directing their men to the designated LCPs.

To me, this didn't appear to be a small maneuver. This looked like something big was going to happen. It was daylight when our turn came to go. There were four navy transport ships distant in the harbor. We were transported to the closest one. I think this time we lucked out. Being the last sometimes is good for the soul. The ship was filled with troops from the bottom up. The first men on got their accommodations down in the hole.

As soon as we boarded the ship, a crewman pointed to a side door, led us down one flight of stairs to a very narrow space with bunks two high against one side of the wall. This must have been a place designed for the ship's crewmen. It was almost private, very good for us, and nobody complained.

It didn't take us long to settle in our new quarters. Each man secured a bunk. This time the latrine and washroom was nearby, which was very handy. After placing our gear on the bunks, we were free to go up on deck to observe this on-going great military maneuver.

On deck it was a beautiful New Caledonia day. Four navy transport ships and several destroyers or escort ships filled the bay. The LCPs manned by sailors were still transporting soldiers and sailors to their designated ships.

Nouméa looked beautiful in the morning sun. St. Joseph's Cathedral, very visible, like an archangel, stood there overlooking the town. I remember when we first got here March 12, and saw the town and the cathedral. Someone said, "This has to be a nice place because good people live here." I found it so.

Time went by very fast. It was already November 7, 1942. Minus a few days, we were in New Caledonia seven months. On deck, some of the guys gathered and told stories about things that happened to them while in New Caledonia. I had a few stories of my own I could tell, but Sid Garret had a real love story we all knew.

He met a girl in Nouméa and fell in love. She was a French girl. She and her mother were white and her sister was black. Sid never met her father. Sid tried to get permission from the army command to marry the girl, but his time waiting ran out.

Sid was very angry at our company commander. He thought he had something to do with him not getting permission to marry the girl. It was a love affair with a sad ending. I liked Joe Bargiel's attitude when he said, "I think I owe a few bucks to the man I was buying my wine from. Oh well, I'll pay him when I see him again."

I thought, "Yeah, sure you will."

Someone asked Art Boessneck if he had anything of interest happen to him while here. He said, "Yeah. I went hunting with a Frenchman. We got a deer."

I liked James Bertie's story the best. I heard it the night it happened. Jim told the guy about the few flings he had with René, the beautiful French, dark-skinned girl we met at the French fort while eating lunch with the French officers after our infamous gun instructions episode.

In her mother's house at the nickel docks, not a very safe place to be at night, Jim and René were enjoying a few glasses of wine in her little bedroom apartment. At times, René sipped on wine and then danced a little and then removed a piece of clothing and flipped it across the room. Jim watched and liked what he saw. She climbed on a small dressing table next to the bed, like a little stage, still dancing, and she took off her last piece of clothing, her panties, and flipped them at Jim.

Jim told the guys he got very excited. He said, "In the dimly lit, glowing light, on that pedestal, René looked like a dancing Hawaiian princess. In bed, leaning on a couple of pillows, I wanted to jump up and grab her. Suddenly, like a dove, she leaped through the air and landed next to me."

Jim ended the story there. He said, "To go on, it would not be fair to René, nor to any other woman I would ever know!"

Some of the guys dismissed anything that happened in New Caledonia between the soldiers and the people as a nothing-nothing episode. Their attitude was, we'll never see this place again, so why worry?

I personally liked the place and the people. In school, I loved geography, and this was geography in real life. I learned a lot from the people I met here, about their life and their culture. I felt I was taking a little bit of what I learned with me, and just maybe, I left a little bit of myself here in Nouméa. I thought someday I might come back. I'd like that.

In the bay, troop and supply movement continued for most of the day.

I learned something I didn't know before. When we left the U.S. we were a part of Task Force 6814 P. Now we became part of a newly formed division called the Americal. I guess the name was derived from American army units being gathered in New Caledonia. Americal Division: a very nice name.

6. Company on the Move

It was already getting dark when the transport pulled anchor and started slowly moving out to sea. The navy escort ships were first to leave the bay, and the three troop transports farthest out followed. Our ship was the last to leave. By the time we cleared the bay, the transport ships and the town of Nouméa disappeared in the dark. Leaning on the ship's railing, I said goodbye to New Caledonia and said a prayer for what was coming next.

A troop ship's blackout meant no lights of any kind on this ship's decks at night, and don't ever light a cigarette if you want to live, but all of us world travelers knew that from previous voyages.

I slept on deck that night with the rest of my buddies. In the morning, we counted four troop transports and four or more navy escort ships so far out you could hardly see them. At times it looked as if they disappeared underwater, and then they would appear again.

Our ship's routine was two meals a day, in line, take your turn at the latrine and shower and make sure you fill your canteen with fresh water for the day.

The decks were forever occupied by guys playing cards, dozing off, or writing letters. I wrote a letter home. I thought, this could be my last chance to write a letter home for now, or this could be the very last letter I write. I wanted this to sound like a casual letter, yet I managed to tell my mother how much I loved her, and I thanked my father for showing me how to be a man.

In the morning of our third day, on deck the front and rear battery gunners fired their anti-aircraft guns. Art Boessneck, our artillery expert, explained the gunners were testing the guns, making sure they were in working condition, just in case they needed them. We also saw sailors mounting machine guns on the deck and the landing craft.

The army chaplains seemed to be everywhere talking to the guys. Losing sense of time while on these army-navy cruises was common. Someone wanted to know if this was our fifth night and fourth day sailing, or was this our fourth day and fifth night coming up?

Jim Bertie had the answer. He said, "Today is November 11, 1942." With sarcasm he added, "Last night was our fourth night and today is our fourth day aboard this luxury liner." Nobody laughed.

That afternoon we spotted more ships on the horizon. They were transport ships going in the same direction.

Lieutenant Ben Rabin gathered the guys together and told us the ships that joined our convoy were troop ships from New Hebrides going to the same place we were. He told us if things worked out well, tomorrow morning we were going to be making a landing on the island of Guadalcanal.

He said, "The 1st and 2nd Marines and the 5th and 7th Marine regiments including the army's of 164th Infantry regiment are holding a good part of the island surrounding Henderson Airfield. We'll have plenty to do." Then he told us to be ready tomorrow morning to disembark by climbing down the side of the ship on the rope net ladders into Higgins boats, the LCPs.

He said, "There might be some opposition from the Japanese, but we should be all right. Let's try to stay together when we hit the beach."

That evening a prayer service was held on the upper deck, and it seemed everyone on board was there. The chaplain led the men in prayer and then talked for a long time about love of family, love of our country, and of freedom and love of God. Then he pondered the reasons why sometimes young men are chosen to go into battle to keep their freedoms free.

When I was leaving home after my last five day leave, my mother handed me a small pocket sized booklet and said, "I want you to keep this booklet with you. It's the Novena prayer to our Lady of the Miraculous Medal. Read the prayer every day. I'll do the same." She then placed a golden chain with a sky blue miraculous medal around my neck. The medal was beautiful. I had never seen one like that before. She had tears in her eyes, yet she was trying to smile.

She said, "I know you'll come back. I'll beg her every day."

I kissed my mother goodbye and told her, "Please don't worry, Mom, I'll be back."

I tried to read the Novena prayer every day. Later it became a habit and in time I could recite the prayer by heart. That night, I recited the Novena prayer twice, maybe even three times and in my thoughts I kissed my mother's cheek and gave my father a hug.

I don't think anyone slept that night. The infantry battalion on board took up most of the deck space. They were in full combat gear. Our group took a small area on the front deck. Lt. Rabin urged the guys to get some sleep, but I didn't see him getting any sleep either.

The only action I heard during the night was guys running to the johns, then coming back to their same resting places. I don't think breakfast was served that morning. I know I didn't eat anything.

6. Company on the Move

At the very beginning, the ship's crewmen were busy releasing the prefixed net like rope ladders down the sides of the ship and mounting the Higgins boats to the crane lowering hoists. When they started checking the machine guns, I wanted to go over and check them myself to make sure they worked.

In the very far distance we could see land on both sides of the ship. The convoy's ships were much closer together. It seemed they were forming a formation, one ship after another, and ready to sail between the islands.

7.

Guadalcanal

According to Lt. Rabin, we were entering Iron Bottom Sound, a graveyard for sunken ships, a large body of water between Savo Island and Tulagi Island and Guadalcanal. Our convoy was headed for Guadalcanal. At first the island looked like a large cloud of mist, and then as we got closer in the early morning sunlight almost mysteriously it turned green and we could see beautiful palm trees and sandy beaches.

Our ship dropped anchor about six or seven hundred feet away from shore. My first thought was "this looks like a nice place," and I didn't hear any shooting yet.

Instantly, the ship's deck became alive with action. The crewmen started lowering the Higgins boats into the water. The infantry battalion's officers and sergeants shouted orders to their men to climb down the rope ladders into the landing crafts. The rope ladders fastened to the ship railing were about ten feet wide, permitting four or five men to climb down at a time into the landing craft followed by other men right behind. As soon as the landing craft was full with men, it headed for the beach at full speed, and another landing craft took its place at the bottom of the ladder.

Without stopping, the infantry battalion, company after company, disembarked the ship using several ladder installations. The entire procedure was very professional, very orderly, and fast. And then it was our turn to go. When I climbed over the railing and started down the ladder I heard someone holler, "Alex, look up!" I looked up. Jim Bertie snapped my picture going down the ladder. That was the last time I saw Jim Bertie for the next week or so. I must have been one of the last guys to get in that landing craft because immediately it took off for the beach. When I looked around, maybe a dozen guys from our group were on the landing craft, and the rest were left on the ship.

7. Guadalcanal

Troops disembarking ship by rope ladder into landing craft during air bombardment, Guadalcanal, November 12, 1942.

Three other troop ships were anchored nearby. Sailors operating the landing craft were all over the place moving men and supplies.

Someone said, "We are landing at Lunga Point."

The beach was now filled with troops, boxes of supplies and 50 gallon barrels filled with gasoline and oil. The barrels were dropped off the ships' decks into the water and floated. The island's native men swam behind the barrels and floated them into the beach. We later learned they were given a can of bully beef for every barrel they swam into shore.

Our landing craft hit the beach and dropped its front exit ramp. As we ran off the landing craft, I think I heard sirens first, and then someone on a loudspeaker shouted, "Condition Red. Clear the beaches." I believe the ship's gunners opened with anti-aircraft fire first. Almost instantly, Japanese Zeros appeared flying at treetop level with machine guns spraying bullets along the beach.

We all ran toward the palm trees. Conrad Tenant ran first. I was right behind him. He kept shouting, "Hit the dirt!" but kept running. I ran with him. When we hit the dirt I was lying right next to a 50 gallon barrel of gasoline, and the other guys were there with me. The gunfire stopped for a moment. When I got up to see what happened and looked across the beach, I saw the ships were turning around and heading for open waters.

Within moments, anti-aircraft guns from all directions started firing again.

The Japanese dive bombers were attacking our moving ships. Immense gunfire from ships and land countered the bombers. Some of the dive bombers never came out of the dive. They hit the water and exploded. Others came out of the dive but were hit, and then flew some and went down in flames. None of the bombs dropped hit any of our ships.

The ships were on the move when another group of dive bombers appeared, but this time, from somewhere U.S. fighter planes met them head on. I saw at least three Japanese bombers shot down by our fighter planes. Because of gunfire and shrapnel coming from the sky, several times we had to run for cover and jump into the ditches. Once Sid Garret jumped on top of me and almost broke my arm.

Our ships vanished into the horizon. Later we learned the ships were informed of the coming air attack and were ordered to leave the area. The beach became alive with activity again. The boxes of supplies were carried inland on small army trucks.

7. Guadalcanal

Landing beach, Guadalcanal, 1942.

The native men were rolling the gasoline and oil barrels off the beaches into the tree line. The infantry men that were on board ship with us disappeared into the brush. Our little group gathered together, and we counted heads, "Two, four, six, ten, twelve, anyone else? Where are the rest of the guys? Didn't they get off the ship?"

Lieutenant Rabin, Sgt. DeBoni, and my good buddy Jim Bertie and a few others didn't get off the ship. I wondered what happened. I hoped they were okay. A couple of our guys walked down the beach a little ways hoping to find some of our group lost, but no such luck.

When the ships sped away, they left their Higgins boats stranded on the beaches. Walking the beach, several men with large white patches on their arms, Beach Patrol, approached each boat and talked to the crewmen, probably giving them some kind of instructions.

When the patrol men saw us, they came over and wanted to know who we were and why we were there. After a lengthy conversation, when they finally understood we were ordnance men, they suggested we go to a Marine outpost about a thousand feet from the beach, close to Henderson Field.

They said, "The Seabees are also there. Somebody will take you in.

You'll find food and shelter there." They also told us a large Japanese armada was headed this way, that this might be the night of nights to remember, if our navy showed up ... and if they didn't show up, well....

"When you get to the muddy road, turn left."

Slowly, we walked in the direction the men had pointed. Some of the palm trees had no tops and some of the trees were lying on their sides, destroyed by artillery shells. There were coconuts all over the ground. Later we learned this place was called the Coconut Grove, owned by the Libby Soap Company, and for each tree destroyed, the U.S. Government had to pay the company a hundred dollars.

We found the road. It was all mud. We could see Henderson Field, and to the left we could see tents concealed by trees and bushes.

Bomb and shell holes covered the side of the road. Apparently the area close to Henderson Field was bombed and shelled many times and was not a good place to be during a raid. We entered the camp. To me, this didn't look like a small outpost. It looked like some kind of command post. At least a dozen tents were scattered among the coconut trees and each tent had its own air raid shelter covered with coconut logs and coral sand. A large canvas flap covered what looked like a mess hall stand with men serving food. We stopped at a nearby hanging water bag and started filling our canteens. The water was warm.

A Marine sergeant appeared from somewhere and wanted to know if we were lost. When he heard our story, he told us to wait there. He might be able to help.

The sergeant returned and told us we could stay there in camp until our commanding officers got there.

He informed us the colonel had a truckload of battle scarred weapons that needed repair. He was Master Sergeant Tipper Bronson with the Marine Headquarters Command. He suggested that we get some food at the Marine mess tent and get some rest. According to the information the sergeant had, a forty ship Japanese task force was heading towards Guadalcanal. They would arrive sometime in the night. He emphasized that every capable man on the island would be on the beaches defending our positions. He told us a small detachment of Colonel Carlson's Marine raiders were there with us, going down to the beach before dark. He thought we should join them. He told us he would call us when it was time to go.

We took off our backpacks, placed them next to a tree and went through the chow line. In addition to some canned stew and a piece of

7. Guadalcanal

hardtack, the server tossed two chocolate bars on my mess kit. I had never seen them before. There were six squares of chocolate wrapped in red cellophane paper. You were supposed to eat two squares for breakfast, two for lunch, and two for dinner: a day's ration. I ate the six chocolate squares at one time. My buddies did the same.

One of the guys had a suggestion, "Let's put our personal stuff, billfolds, pictures, etc. in one backpack. If we all come back, no problem, but if some don't, the ones that did will make sure the others' stuff is mailed to his family."

All of us agreed it was a good idea. All I had was a billfold with a few small pictures, my ID card and a few bucks. I don't think anyone had that much more than that. Everything went into one backpack.

The late afternoon sun was very hot. Someone remarked the temperature at Henderson Field was 120 degrees. I didn't think it was much cooler where we were. Everybody was tired. In a shady spot, leaning against a tree, I fell asleep. When I woke up and looked around, we were surrounded by young men standing and sitting in groups talking out loud.

I believe they were the Marines the other sergeant was telling us about. They were very young. They looked like high school seniors. They all had rifles, but what I noticed a little bit different was some of them had bolo knives hanging from their belts, and I wondered where they got them. I didn't think that was standard issue.

The Marine who seemed to be in charge of this group didn't have any rank markings on him at all, but when he spoke, the young fellows listened. I tried to hear what he was saying but all I heard was, "If they get to the beach, we'll cut them down."

What happened next was amazing. There were no loud orders, no formation, no shouting, no noise of any kind, and yet, the young Marines were gone. They vanished. One of our guys asked, "Where did they go?" The sergeant we talked to first came over and said, "I talked to the Marine captain. He accepted you into his group. Why didn't you guys go with them?"

Someone said, "We didn't know. Nobody told us."

The sergeant seemed a bit perturbed. He probably remembered he told us he would call us. He said, "Go back to the beach; you'll find them there. The Japs are coming sometime tonight. By the way, the password for tonight is 'Lillian.' Don't forget."

The Japanese couldn't pronounce the letter "L." It was a good password, and how could I forget "Lillian"? It was my sister's name.

585 Raids and Counting

When we got to the beach, it was getting dark. Off the beach, about 25 feet into the brush was a trench extending along the shoreline covered with bomb and shell craters. At a distance I could see a 155mm Longton artillery piece aimed at the ocean. There were four such artillery pieces along the beach. Marines and soldiers filled the trench and foxholes, some manning .50 and .30 caliber machine guns.

Somebody hollered at us, "Get in the trench!"

Since the trench was pretty well filled, I looked for a spot and jumped in between two Marines. One, a very young Marine, wanted to know if I had any hand grenades on me.

I said, "No."

He said, "Don't bother with your rifle. When the Japs come up the beach, pull the pin and throw the grenade, but don't forget to duck after you throw one." I thought his advice was good, even though I was a pretty good shot with a rifle, but in the dark, a grenade would, no doubt, cover more ground. It was about 10 P.M. and all you could hear was the water swishing along the beach, and the biggest, brightest moon I ever saw in my life lit up the place. It was so bright I could read the serial numbers on my rifle. I didn't know if the light was good or bad for us. This was going to be my first battle. I was kind of praying it wasn't going to be my last one.

Just a little ways inland, a small hut was used as a radio communication center, from which we were getting hourly reports about how far out the Japanese naval armada was. The last report indicated the Japs were about ten miles out, coming in fast. The guys in the trenches had one question: "Good God, where is our navy?"

I just looked at my watch. It was exactly 11 P.M. when I saw what looked like a light flying from one side of the horizon to the other side near Savo Island. One light flying after another, like aircraft flying off of an aircraft carrier. I never knew, at night, in the dark, you could see artillery shells fly through the air. The battle for Guadalcanal had begun.

When the battleships, cruisers, and destroyers opened fire on both sides, the island of Guadalcanal rocked. The sky at the horizon lit up red and orange and purple from exploding artillery shells, bombs and torpedoes. The explosions created a wave of booming sounds so great you could not only hear it, but you could also feel it, like a wind across your face. At times the earth moved and vibrated under our feet. At first, all of us dropped to the bottom of the trench and hugged the sand, but no artillery

7. Guadalcanal

shells came our way. Everybody got out of the trenches and foxholes and hundreds of us, Marines and soldiers watched one of the greatest navy battles of the Pacific.

In the very early dawn's light, two Japanese troop transport ships were making their way towards Tassaronga Point. From somewhere, a squadron of U.S. diver bombers appeared and encountered the Japs' ships under enormous antiaircraft fire. The planes peeled off from one another and went into a dive over the ships, releasing their bombs and then coming out of their dive under severe gunfire and flying away. The ships were severely damaged. All of the U.S. planes got away. The men in the trenches watching the maneuver cheered the planes as if watching a ballgame.

The four 155mm Long Toms on shore opened fire and received credit for helping sink two of the Jap transport ships. Badly damaged from bombs and artillery shells, one ship went down to the bottom of Iron Bottom Sound and the other ship ran up on shore at Tassaronga Point. The Marines fired their guns at the small boats and rafts left in the water.

Later that morning we learned the results of the battle as reported by

Disabled Japanese troop ship beached during night battle, Guadalcanal, November 12 and 13, 1942.

585 Raids and Counting

that small radio receiving station. U.S. admiral William F. Halsey was there waiting for the Japanese. His naval force included the battleships *Washington* and *South Dakota*, the aircraft carrier *Enterprise*, several cruisers and about twenty destroyers.

The Japanese force included four battleships, two aircraft carriers, *Jungo* and *Hiejo*, about eight cruisers, 28 destroyers, and 11 troop transport ships.

The U.S. Navy lost two cruisers, *Atlanta* and *Juneau*, and seven destroyers. The battleship *South Dakota* was slightly damaged.

The Japanese lost two battleships, *Hiei* and *Kirishima*, one cruiser, the *Kinugasa*, a couple of destroyers and seven troop transports. Their troop loss had to be great.

There was no count of aircraft lost on either side.

The Marines moved out of the trenches. I think my young Marine friend was disappointed. I didn't have to use any of his grenades. He gave me a very friendly handshake and said, "Maybe there will be another time?"

Clouds gathered over the island and rain came down in deluge form, as if shedding tears out loud for the men who last night and this morning lost their lives in battle.

By the time our group gathered, we were soaking wet. We took a head count and one of our guys was missing: Joe Bargiel. We all looked up and down the beach and in the trench and in the bomb craters, but no Joe. Our rumor king was gone. We waited, and while we were trying to come up with a search strategy to find Joe, suddenly the need ended. That very moment I wished I had a camera or a good artist or cartoonist there who could have recorded that stunning picture.

Joe Bargiel walked out of the thickest part of the brush with rain water dripping down his face. His rifle was strung over his shoulder and he carried his helmet in his left hand. In his right hand he held up high his army mess kit and in it was the biggest piece of Spam I ever saw.

When he got to our group, he put the mess kit on the ground and asked, "Who's got a knife?"

Every one of us asked Joe, "Where were you?"

Joe told us he saw the Marines handing out pieces of Spam to their men. He said, "I got in line and asked for a big piece." Joe managed to cut the Spam up into twelve equal pieces. We all ate the Spam. It was exceptionally good.

The rain slowed down to a sprinkle. The beach became active with

7. Guadalcanal

men moving cargo supplies left there from yesterday's departed ships. We stood there waiting, maybe, for some higher power to guide us. All great technicians, able to make old cannons fire and automatic weapons exhale thousands of rounds and battle search instruments to perform their duties excellently, and we waited, but no such guidance came.

Since we had no ranking officer to give us orders, we were not attached to any unit on the island, we had no home and no place to call our own. The decision to go back to the Marine post was unanimous. Besides, our stuff was there. We had but one question, "Who knows how to get back there?"

We walked along the beach and tried to stay out of the way of the soldiers and native men still clearing cargo supplies from the beach. I was still impressed by the way the native men swam the drums of gasoline from ship to shore. If the natives hadn't been there, I wondered who would have done that job.

When we turned into the coconut grove, I thought we had walked too far because we couldn't find the muddy road or see the airfield. We were too far north or south or somewhere.

The guys were arguing about the trees, that the place we were at didn't look like the place we were looking for. To me, all the coconut trees looked alike.

I wondered why the guys were so concerned about the trees and where we were going and nobody said anything about what happened last night and early this morning. This November, 11–12–13, would go down in history as dates for one of the greatest naval battles fought in the South Pacific for Guadalcanal and the Solomon Islands.

The guys leading our little parade stopped. For some reason all of us turned towards the ocean and kept looking at the clear water licking the beach, as if to verify what we saw last night and this morning really happened. We were there. A little bit of rain and a little bit of sunshine, all in all, for us it was a beautiful morning.

One of the guys broke the silence and said, "What we saw last night and this morning, someday people will read about in books, and we're still here. Thank God."

Everybody said, "Yeah, thank God."

I believe it was Sid Garrett that asked, "When the Marines opened fire at the life rafts left there from the sinking Jap troop ships, did any of you guys fire your rifles?"

585 Raids and Counting

Nobody answered Sid's question. I wondered why. I knew when the young Marine started shooting at the rafts out in the ocean I was lying next to him at the top of the trench with my rifle in my arms. Did I really fire my rifle? I didn't answer Sid's question either.

Somebody said, "Let's go."

We kept on walking through the coconut grove.

I think we all saw the old truck at the same time. In a very wooded and overgrown spot, we saw the front end of a very old truck. It was well rusted, and the cab had no doors or windshield. It was a flatbed truck. It had all the tires, and to me, it looked like someone backed it into the bushes not long ago and tried to hide it.

I thought it was a great find, and said, "Let's try to get it started. If it starts, we'll ride."

I was the big loser, everyone agreed it was a Jap truck. To me it looked like something the native workers used to haul coconuts with.

There was no key for the ignition. It was replaced by a switch. Two very suspicious wires hung from behind the dashboard. Everybody's remarks were, "Touch the two wires together, the thing will blow sky high!"

My thought was, "Why would anyone want to wire a piece of junk like this?"

The ground was covered with palm tree branches. I picked up several branches and put them over the truck's hood, concealing its appearance. I told the guys, "I'm coming back to get this truck." They laughed.

We found the muddy road, the Marine camp, and our backpacks exactly where we left them. A group of men was unloading boxes from a small military truck and stacking them next to the would be kitchen.

We could hear tractors or bulldozers working at the airfield. We were wet and hungry. We started discussing what do we do next when sirens went off, condition red. The marine camp became alive with men running from the tents to their air raid shelters, and that very second our anti-aircraft guns opened fire. All of us fell to the ground.

I tried to look up. Somebody hollered, "There they are," and a sound I never heard in my life, like two giants ripping a heavy piece of carpet, and then bombs exploding on the airfield. Apparently, the bombs were intended to destroy the runway to keep our aircraft from operating from there. The entire episode from start to finish lasted less than five minutes.

Now we knew why the Marine camp air raid shelters were built with

7. Guadalcanal

a roof of coconut logs, sandbags, sand and coral. The shrapnel in the air from exploding antiaircraft shells has to come down and it's much better if you're under cover. Once you hear the roar of bombs flying over your head, you will never forget it. Everyone had a different description what the falling bombs sound was like — like a rain gone by, or a plane in a deep dive or a ripping sound. I never heard giants ripping carpet, but that's what I thought it sounded like.

Soon we found out and realized how great our brothers, the Marines, were to us, and Master Sergeant Tipper Bronson was the greatest. He was from Kentucky. He joined the Marines when he was seventeen years old and just completed his eighteenth year in the service, and he loved every minute of it.

He said, "You men have the colonel's approved order to use this camp as your temporary quarters. Use the mess hall and all sanitary facilities." He told us the muddy road was the lifeline to the men on the island. It connected the airfield, the beaches, the first aid station, and Lunga Point, the river. He pointed a little ways to a spot along the road and made a suggestion.

He said, "That would be a good place for your company to build your ordnance camp. You'll need the road." He also suggested we choose a spot along the road for our future tent location and start digging some air raid shelters before the day was over. He said, "We get two or three air raids a night, sometimes more. I'll get you guys some shovels."

We broke up into three groups. Joe Bargiel, Ralph Clark, Sid Garret, and I chose a spot along the right side of the road at a small opening, a good place for a tent, and started digging an air raid shelter.

The ground was very hard, mostly coral and tree roots, and very hard to dig. Stripped to the waist, we took turns digging with shovel and pick. We tried to copy the shelters we saw at the Marine camp. After three or four hours of digging we had a hole dug about six feet long by four feet wide and about three feet deep. It had to be deeper.

Our guys on the other side of the road had the same problem. Their coral was no softer than ours.

It started to rain again. In our backpacks we had no rain gear. I had a half of a pup tent, some underwear, a razor and toothbrush, a mess kit, a first aid packet, my tool kit, and a pack of cigarettes.

All of us decided against building pup tents; instead we used each half of the tent as a rain poncho. That was a good decision because the

585 Raids and Counting

rain kept coming down. Overhead was the constant sound of U.S. dive bombers flying from our aircraft carriers; they were very active attacking the damaged Japanese ships from last night's battle around Savo Island. We later learned a Japanese battleship, *Hiei*, severely damaged, sank there.

On the other side of Henderson Field, our field artillery kept pounding the Japanese. The firing would stop for a while and then start all over again.

Late that afternoon we went through the Marine chow line. It was our first meal of the day, not counting Joe's pieces of Spam. We listened to the Marines talk.

One of the guys serving chow was Barney Ross, a very famous lightweight boxer from New York. During a Japanese shelling, he pulled a wounded Marine into a shelter and saved his life. He received a hero's medal for that.

We learned from the Marines, "Don't light a cigarette in the dark while sitting on a foxhole, and don't answer to somebody calling, 'Hey, Joe! Where are you?' It's not a friend."

That night we made camp at our unfinished pre-dug shelters. I thought sitting next to a coconut tree would be better than trying to sleep lying down on the wet ground. I leaned against a tree and covered myself with the pup tent poncho. Ralph Clark did the same. Joe Bargiel couldn't find a comfortable way to sit or sleep. He kept talking about what kind of bed he would buy when he got home.

I don't know if any of us slept any or not. During the night there were three Condition Reds. Each time the Japanese planes approached the island, first the anti-aircraft shells burst into the air and then you could hear the bombs fall, that ripping sound. Most of the bombs were aimed at the airfield and planes if any were there, but bombs can fall anywhere.

Each time we jumped into our unfinished shelter and stayed there until the raid was over. After the third raid, we stayed in the shelter. Sitting on wet coral really wasn't that bad. I had the poncho on my head. It kept the drizzle from my face and my buddies were nearby. What else could I ask for? If I had one wish for right now, I thought, what would I wish for? Maybe a dry stool to sit on, or maybe a large umbrella big enough to cover all of us? My shins were itching pretty bad and I scratched. I wondered what my dear mother would say or do if she saw me now.

At the very early break of dawn, at the far side of Henderson Field, our artillery batteries started shelling the Japanese ground positions. Each

7. Guadalcanal

firing barrage lasted for a few minutes, stopped, then started all over again. It went on and on and on. According to the information we had about our ground positions, the Marines and army units were holding on to about four square miles of the island.

Last night's bombing raids convinced all of us our air raid shelters were far from being finished. If we intended to pitch our company camp here, between the beach and Henderson Field, the most bombed and shelled spot on the island, we had to dig the shelters deeper and reinforce the tops with coconut logs, sandbags, and coral sand.

Coconut trees, in pieces, destroyed by Japanese Navy artillery shellings, were everywhere. The U.S. Navy Seabees, while clearing the airfield, stacked broken logs into piles. All we had to do was carry or drag them to our shelters.

Somehow, Joe Bargiel became the group's great organizer. He had the knack for picking jobs.

He said, "Why don't half of us stay here and dig the shelters deeper, and the other half go get the logs?"

Everybody said, "I'll dig."

"How the hell are we going to get the logs here?" someone said, "They're too damn heavy to carry."

Someone said, "We'll roll them or pull them." There was no end to the stupid suggestions.

In my opinion, there was no way we were going to carry, pull, or roll the logs. There had to be a better way. I remembered the truck we found in the weeds, somewhere between here and the beach. I knew I could find it.

"Joe, I'm going to go get that truck we found," I said, "If I get it started, we'll have the logs with no problem."

At first nobody said a word, then Joe Bargiel said, "Alex, go get the truck."

I waved my hand in an "okay" motion to Joe, and asked Ralph Clark if he would go with me. I don't know who was the first one to call me stupid.

Sid Garrett said, "You're some kind of stupid nut. If you go, you'll blow yourself up. Give me your cigarettes. I know you're not coming back."

Everybody liked Ralph Clark. He was a good friend. Everybody called him Ronald. He carried his girlfriend's picture with him at all times. We all saw her picture many times. The guys knew she was beautiful. She looked like Betty Grable in the movies. Ronald loved her.

One of the guys said, "Yeah, Ronald, give me your girl's picture. If you go with that nut you'll not need it anymore."

Ralph Clark and I walked toward the beach and tried to keep to the overgrown part of the coconut grove because that's how I remembered where we saw the truck. The place looked isolated, maybe because of the fallen trees. When you left the muddy road, you were on your own.

We saw a wild parrot resting in a treetop. He was large and very colorful. When we got closer he made a very loud laughing sound, enough to send chills up your back. He flew away.

We found the truck. It was in the same spot, not moved. The branches I placed on the front of the truck were still there. We took the branches off and threw them aside.

Again and again, Ralph and I looked for something that looked out of place or rigged in any way. There was absolutely nothing in or around the motor or under the truck that looked suspicious. We traced the two hanging wires. They went to a light switch, but there were no headlamps. I pulled the two wires from the switch and threw them away.

We checked the wheels to see if a field mine might be set under a tire. There were no field mines under the tires. The gas tank was built in front of the cab over the engine. I stuck a small branch into the gas tank to check the gas level. It was half full.

The truck's steering wheel was on the left side of the cab. The battery was mounted on the running board on the passenger side of the cab. We traced the battery wires to the battery charger and the starter. Everything looked to be in order.

I sat down on the seat behind the steering wheel, pushed the clutch in with my left foot and pulled the gearshift out of gear. I looked at the starter button. It was on the floor, just like my 1934 Ford I had before I was drafted. All I had to do was step on the button. I knew where it was.

Ralph Clark got into the cab and sat down. We sat there for a time. I think I said a prayer, and I had a thought: just in case, why should two of us be in this cab?

I said, "Ronald, if that battery is up, I'm sure this thing is going to start, but just in case, maybe you should go stand behind a coconut tree while I give it a try."

Ronald didn't hesitate to answer. He said, "I'm staying here. Start this damn thing."

7. Guadalcanal

I turned the starter switch to on and stepped on the starter. The engine turned over. The battery was alive.

On the dashboard I pulled out the choke and stepped on the starter again. The engine turned over several times, and then the miracle occurred: the engine started! Both of us jumped! We looked at each other and Ralph grabbed my hand and really shook it. He was excited. I was too.

With my left foot I pushed the clutch pedal down to the floorboard and slipped the gearshift in what I thought was the first gear, and slowly let up the clutch pedal. The truck moved. Slowly I drove the truck out of the thick brush into a small opening. This dumb thing ran a lot better than it looked. Somebody took good care of this ancient vehicle.

For a moment I wondered, "Was this my good luck at work, or was the Good Lord giving us a much needed helping hand?" Most likely the latter was true.

To get the truck moving through the jungle, Ralph and I had to move fallen branches and tree stumps out of our way and look out for bombed out shell holes. When we reached what was called the Coconut Grove, Ralph, standing on the truck's small running board, pointed the way to the clearest path he could see and I managed to keep the truck moving at his direction. The truck had a sound of its own. It was a little bit loud. Maybe it wasn't the sound you wanted your car to have while driving down the street in your hometown, but here in the jungle, who cared?

Moving slowly, we found our way back to our would be camp area. The guys were still digging the air raid shelters, but there were no logs of any kind nearby. I wondered what happened to the work detail assigned to bring in the needed logs.

I drove the truck onto the muddy road, stopped, took the truck out of gear and left the engine running. Ralph and I just sat there. My dear buddies gathered around the truck; some of them touched it. It was as if they had seen something appear to them out of another world. A few guys got on the truck's flatbed and jumped around. Everybody was talking.

They asked, "Did you find any explosives? How did you get it started? How does it drive?"

Joe Bargiel got the guys' attention. "All right, you guys," he shouted. He pointed his hand in one direction and said, "The logs are over there. Let's go get them." He looked at Ralph and me and said, "What took you guys so long?" He smiled, patted me on my shoulder and said, "Wow! Good job!"

585 Raids and Counting

The "muddy" road between Lunga Point, Henderson Field and the 1st Marine Division Headquarters, Guadalcanal, 1942.

We picked out the suitable logs, stacked them on the truck's flatbed and hauled them to our dug shelters. We made several trips. By evening we had the shelters finished, covered with logs, sandbags, and coral. The truck was a blessing at that time and our only possession. We parked it nearby.

Coconuts fallen from trees in their heavy husks were all over the ground. We were hungry. We used our shovels and picks to crack the husks to get the coconut meat. It was good. We ate.

There was a little bit of activity on the muddy road between the airfield and the Marine Headquarters. A few small Marine or Seabee trucks drove by. Some of them stopped and looked at us and wondered, "Who are those guys, and what are they doing here?"

It was getting dark and it started to rain again. All of us were tired, wet, and dirty, but our work was done and it was time to rest.

Two of our guys gathered our canteens, walked over to the Marine camp and filled them with water. They returned with some suggestions from Sgt. Tipper Bronson. "Set up a guard. After dark, sitting in the open, sit back to back, and don't light any cigarettes. If you hear someone calling,

7. Guadalcanal

"Hey, Joe, where are you? Don't answer. It's not your friend." We had heard that before.

In Tennessee, on army maneuvers, we slept in pup tents on the ground. We had blankets and most of the time we were there the weather was dry. On this godforsaken place, it rained all the time, at least since we got there. Each one of us had an idea how best to bed down. I tried to roll up in my half of the pup tent and tried to keep the rain and mosquitoes out of my face. It worked. I fell asleep.

The ground shook. I jumped. I couldn't tell if it was the sound of flying shells, the exploding artillery shells, or the Condition Red siren at the airfield that came first. Four of us scrambled to the shelter at the same time. The shrill sound of the shells flying over our heads was ripping the air. A barrage of shells exploded in rapid succession. The Japanese were shelling Henderson Field with large cannon. The explosions shook the ground, and the sand and coral packed above the coconut logs slipped down into the shelter. I remembered to open my mouth during a shelling to save my eardrums from bursting. The shelling lasted for a short while, stopped, and then started again.

When it was over, we got out of the shelter. Smoke and the smell of gunpowder, a sulfur smell, filled the air. At Henderson Field we could see a large fire. It was either a Seabees (Construction Battalion) heavy piece of equipment, an airplane, or barrels of gasoline burning.

Just before dawn we heard an enormous amount of artillery fire, flying aircraft, and bombardment out at Iron Bottom Sound. In the morning we learned it was the Japanese Navy that did the shelling of Henderson Field while trying to land troops for their much needed reinforcements, west of Tassafaronga. Planes from our aircraft carriers attacked the Japanese. That's the battle we heard during the very early dawn. The Japs lost four troop landing ships and a large number of men in the conflict. We won that battle, and it stopped raining.

This turned out to be one of our better days. We went through the Marine chow line and had some powdered scrambled eggs, powdered mashed potatoes, some hard tack and black coffee. A young Marine standing next to the coffee pot handed each man going through the chow line a small brown pill.

"Take the pill," he said, "It's Atabrine. It will prevent you from catching malaria." We all took the pill. I wished he had a pill to keep the mosquitoes away.

We were sitting in a small circle eating our breakfast and talking about the night's shelling. When I looked up Sgt. Bronson was standing there looking at us. He said, "You guys look terrible. You need a shower and a shave. Do you have any clean clothes?"

Someone said, "No, we haven't."

The sergeant put up his hand in a stay put position and walked away. What happened next was a small miracle, an answer to a prayer. We didn't know by whose order, maybe it was the colonel, a Marine supply sergeant issued all of us some clean clothes. I received underwear, a Marine fatigue jacket, a pair of pants, socks and a pair of new shoes. We got to take a shower and shave.

When I took off my shoes and socks for the first time since we left New Caledonia, some skin came off with the socks. All of us had red blotches on our shins.

The sergeant said, "It's the rain and the heat and it itches like hell. Everybody has it. It's called jungle rot."

We were still getting dressed when a Marine lieutenant came and said something to the sergeant, then asked us if we were the army ordnance men. Joe Bargiel answered, "Yes, sir."

I think the lieutenant repeated the same thing Sergeant Tipper Bronson said to us the first time we saw him. He said, "The colonel has a truckload of battle scarred weapons to repair."

The lieutenant said, "Most of these weapons were picked up in the field after a battle. After you fix and clean them up, they will be reissued again." Then he asked us, "Where is your workshop at?"

We told the lieutenant we had no workshop and no gun parts; all we had was field work kits and some hand tools. There were only five of us here from the small arms section, men that worked on this kind of weapons, but everybody would help. We told him we needed some gun cleaning solvent and gun oil, but any kind of oil would do.

The lieutenant said, "I know I can get you the oil."

We went back to our shelters where our backpacks were, dropped off our dirty clothes and picked up our tools. The old truck was there basking in the morning sun. I was looking at the old truck. I thought, what a wonderful workbench that truck's flatbed would make. Since the battle scarred guns were near the road, we'd have no problem to get the truck there. Everybody agreed.

Someone hollered, "Let's ride!"

7. Guadalcanal

The truck started. I drove the truck to the gun pile and backed it in against the flap top tent. We first started working on the machine guns. We formed an assembly line work system. The guns were brought out of the tent and placed on the truck's flatbed. The small arms men did the checking. Most of the guns were in good working order. All they needed were some adjustments and a good cleaning. The damaged guns we put aside. Later we were going to disassemble them and use the good parts.

A Marine brought a five gallon gas tank full of oil and said, "I got this from the Navy Seabees. I think it's motor oil."

Our dirty undershirts came in handy. Soaked in oil, we used them to clean the guns and oil them at the same time.

By late afternoon we were done with the machine guns. We didn't count them, but I believe there were about fifty very clean, well oiled, very serviceable machine guns stored in the flap tent in a very orderly fashion.

That night we had three Condition Reds, one raid after another. The Jap planes flew in one at a time. They were picked up in the floodlights, blasted with anti-aircraft fire, dropped their bombs and flew away. Each raid lasted about ten or fifteen minutes, but the sound of our anti-aircraft guns blasting the shells exploding in the air, and bombs screeching through the night sky and exploding on the ground, penetrated your entire body. None of us slept too well that night.

That morning when we went back to work on the battle scarred rifles, we found a disaster waiting to happen. Many of the rifles had live ammunition in the gun chambers, bolts closed, ready to be fired. Apparently, the guns picked up on the battlefield were never checked.

We formed a security line and with great care checked each weapon for live ammunition and disarmed it. We separated the working rifles from the ones needing repairs, cleaned and oiled the good ones and stacked them in orderly piles by make, ready to be issued again. The guns needing repairs we put aside to be repaired when we got the parts.

Our contact, the Marine lieutenant, told us the colonel in charge of the weapons supplies was coming to inspect our work and he wanted to talk to us. The colonel came, looked and seemed pleased with what he saw.

He told us we did good work, but we needed more tent space to keep the fixed weapons dry. He was going to have his men put up a few tent flaps for us as soon as he could find the flaps.

We told him about the live ammunition we found in the guns and what a danger it created to handle them.

585 Raids and Counting

R E S T R I C T E D

HEADQUARTERS
AMERICAL DIVISION
APO 716

31 December 1943

GENERAL ORDERS)
NO. 67)   E X T R A C T

AWARDS OF THE PRESIDENTIAL UNIT CITATION

By direction of the President, and authority contained in paragraph 5, Letter, War Department, The Adjutant General's Office, AG 200.6 (29 Jul 43), subject: Eligibility of Army Personnel to the Presidential Unit Citation and ribbon bar with star, dated 5 November 1943, and 1st Indorsement, Headquarters USAFISPA, APO 502, AG 200.6 (7)1, dated 10 December 1943, the Presidential Unit Citation is awarded to the following-named officers and enlisted men of the Americal Division who served in actual combat with the First Marine Division, Reinforced, on Guadalcanal at any time during the period 7 August 1942 to 9 December 1942.

* * *

Tec 4 Alexander A Kunevicius 35011625

* * *

By command of Major General HODGE:

C. M. McQUARRIE
Colonel, General Staff Corps
Chief of Staff

OFFICIAL:

W. H. BIGGERSTAFF
Lieutenant Colonel, Adjutant General's Department
Adjutant General

R E S T R I C T E D

Presidential Unit Citation, awarded for service with the Americal Division on Guadalcanal.

7. Guadalcanal

He assured us he would inform the men in charge of that detail picking up the weapons on the battlefield to correct that problem. Then the colonel gave us an order, sort of. He told us different fighting units would be bringing weapons to us that were needing repairs or needing to be exchanged. If we had what they needed, we were to give it to them, no questions asked, and to repair the weapons they brought in as soon as we got the parts. When the colonel finished talking he kept looking at us as if waiting for an answer.

We all said, "Yes, sir."

The colonel told us he had some machine guns that needed repairs at the airfield; the guns had come out of fighter planes. He wanted to know if any of our men had ever worked on guns that were fired from planes and if they were different in any way.

At first nobody said a word because none of us had ever worked on machine guns that came from planes, but then Joe Bargiel pointed his finger at me and said, "Yes, sir. Alex Kunevicius can fix them."

I gulped.

I had never seen or touched a machine gun that had come out of a fighter plane, but how much different could they be? Besides, I could fix anything.

The colonel said, "Alex, I'll let you know when and where to go."

I said, "Yes, sir."

Before he walked away he looked at the truck and said, "Where did you men get that piece of junk?"

I said, "We found it in the jungle, sir. It's our portable workbench."

The colonel laughed and said, "I might need a ride someday. We might take it to the airfield."

The sound from our field artillery batteries firing at the Japanese land positions never seemed to stop. Our fighter planes patrolling the island flew over the treetops, making the trees quiver and coconuts fall. Condition Red sirens, anti-aircraft fire and bombs falling made for a very exciting morning, and it was still early.

Joe Bargiel was sitting on the truck's flatbed with his legs hanging down one side smoking a cigarette. A coconut fell from the tree and hit him on his knee. Joe jumped, fell and rolled on the ground holding his knee. We were going to take him to the first aid station, but Joe wouldn't go.

8.

Lieutenant Ben Rabin and Men Arrive

Activities on the muddy road increased. Trucks loaded with supplies drove by to Henderson Field, the Marine camp, and to the large Navy Seabees compound where men were working the airfield with their heavy earth moving equipment. Air cover over the airfield, the bay and the beaches was intense. In the distance, we could see soldiers with their backpacks and rifles walking from the beaches to the inner island. While we watched, we reasoned there had to be a ship in the bay.

I don't know who saw them first, but I heard someone holler, "There they are! Jim Bertie, Larry Cox, and Sergeant DeBoni!"

Everybody looked. I looked. Three guys with backpacks on their backs were looking our way. They saw us and were waving their arms.

We greeted the three guys like long lost brothers. They looked tired and lost. Everybody asked them the same question, "How did you find us and where's the rest of the guys?"

Sergeant DeBoni told us they got off the boat sometime that morning, waited on the beach for their stuff to be unloaded, and somebody told them the ordnance men were at the Marine camp and gave them directions.

He said, "Lt. Rabin and the guys are on the beach with all of our equipment barracks bags and tents waiting for transportation and a place to go.

We told the sergeant, "We have a place to build our camp right here, if it's okay with Lt. Rabin, and we have our own transportation. Here it is! Our own truck!"

Sergeant DeBoni looked at the truck, smiled, lifted his hand just a little, pointed his finger at the truck and said, "That's your transportation?"

8. Lieutenant Ben Rabin and Men Arrive

"Sarge," I said, "It's not one of our 6 by 6's, but it runs. I'll drive it to the beach and pick up the guys and equipment."

Everybody said, "Yeah."

Sergeant DeBoni said, "Go ahead. It's okay with me. Take Jim Bertie with you. He'll show you where they are."

Jim jumped in the truck. This was the first time I drove the truck on the dirt road along Henderson Field, the road that led to the beach. It was a short ride, maybe a half mile.

Two transport ships were being unloaded of troops and supplies. Our fighter planes were in the sky over the bay, protecting the ships from a possible Japanese bombing attack.

Since the truck didn't have four wheel drive, I was afraid to drive it on the beach's soft sand. I drove the truck off the road to where the coconut grove started and drove it until we found our group. Lt. Ben Rabin and the men were happy to see us.

I turned the truck around. We loaded the barracks bags, tents, and toolboxes on the flatbed and headed back to the road. Lieutenant Benjamin Rabin sat in the truck with me, some men jumped on the flatbed and some walked behind the truck.

Lt. Rabin asked me, "Where did you get the truck?"

I told him we found it in the jungle. He asked me if any of our men were hurt during the big navy battle. I told him all of our guys were okay. He asked me how come I was wearing a Marine fatigue shirt with U.S. Marines written on the pocket. I told him about the rain, us sleeping in the open, the digging of the air raid shelters, the lack of a change of clothes, and how the Marine colonel took us under his wing. He asked me the colonel's name. I told him I didn't know. I told him the colonel told us to build our camp next to the Marine headquarters. Our camp would be between the beach, Henderson Field, Marine Headquarters, and the Navy Seabees construction battalion, a real strategic place for an ordnance camp to be.

Lt. Rabin said, "We'll see."

When we got back to our would be preordained campsite, the guys spent a little time greeting each other, exchanging stories and inspecting our air raid shelters.

Lieutenant Rabin, Sergeant DeBoni and a few guys were walking around looking over our would-be campsite. It didn't take long for the lieutenant to make a decision.

He called the guys together and said, "This place will make a good ordnance depot. We'll build our camp right here."

The guys broke up into groups, grabbed their barracks bags and tents off the truck, chose a place and started building tents and digging air raid shelters. With the truck we helped the guys move the needed logs for the tops of the shelters.

My tent partners were Joe Bargiel, Ralph Clark, and James Bertie. We built our tent next to the shelter we dug, closest to the road and the Marine camp.

Soon we had pyramidal tents up, scattered among the palm trees, in an area between the muddy road and the airfield. We had our own camp.

We had three Condition Reds that night. Every time the Japanese bombers flew toward the airfield our anti-aircraft guns filled the sky with exploding shells. We shared our air raid shelters with the men that didn't have their shelters finished. Some of the bombs that fell a little bit closer made the ground shake.

Our newly arrived buddies were baptized by the seeping shelter sand, but all and all, it was a good night. We were all there in the morning.

After the night's adventure, the guys finished digging their shelters with great enthusiasm. Lieutenant Rabin met the Marine colonel, whose name I've been unable to retrieve. It appeared the colonel was relieved and glad to turn over the battle scarred weapons to an army ordnance lieutenant and his crew. Lieutenant Rabin must have made a good impression on the colonel. After the meeting, the lieutenant said, "I think the colonel is happy to have us here. I think he just adopted us."

Since our camp was only a few hundred feet from the Marine camp, we used some of their facilities and ate what they ate. Lieutenant Rabin thought it would be better if we moved the repaired weapons supply to our work area, inside our camp, if it was okay with the colonel.

Sergeant DeBoni procured a number of the tent tops from the Seabees. They had everything, and they were very helpful. We strung rope high between the palm trees, flung the tents over the rope and stretched the tents to both sides of the rope, making a nice roof for a good dry work and storage place.

With our old truck, we moved the repaired weapons from the Marine camp to our new work area. One of our guys, using an old dirty board he found, scratched out the letters "22nd Ordnance Company" and tied the board to a palm tree along the road.

8. Lieutenant Ben Rabin and Men Arrive

We were ready to do our part and fix guns. I'm not sure how the word got out that we were there. Very soon weapons needing repairs came from all directions. We repaired or exchanged from stock the guns that were brought in. The badly damaged guns were torn down for parts. In some cases, we made one or two good working guns from three badly damaged ones. Our stock of guns grew.

We found some of the automatic weapons, machine guns, and handguns inoperable because of the island's sand and coral, which were very damaging to any moving parts. In most cases, a good cleaning put those weapons back in service.

At the Marine colonel's instructions, we made a few trips to Henderson Field, picked up machine guns used by navy fighter planes, serviced them, and then took them back to the airfield again.

The airfield was manned by the Marines, the Seabees (Construction Battalion) with their heavy earth moving equipment, forever building and repairing runways, and the naval aviation men who took care of planes that landed there.

We were told that at midday the temperature on the runway would reach about 120 degrees Fahrenheit. We didn't spend too much time there.

This was my third trip driving the old truck to the airfield. Sidney Garrett went with me. We had four well cleaned and serviced machine guns to deliver to the navy men that serviced the planes.

As we approached the airfield, an F4F Wildcat fighter plane was making a landing. Instantly, the Japanese opened artillery fire at the airfield. Sid Garrett jumped from the truck into a ditch. I stopped the truck and jumped, but the shelling stopped as fast as it started. I was okay, but Sid Garrett jumped into a ditch rigged with barbed wire. He received a few bad cuts on his legs. I unloaded the guns while Sid tried to doctor up his wounds.

A navy petty officer wanted to know where we found the old truck. He seemed fascinated by it. I told him we found the truck on the other side of the coconut grove in the bushes.

He said, "Would you like a small good truck for that old heap?" At first I thought he was trying to do us a favor by giving us a better truck, but not so. He soon added, "Would a couple bottles of 7 Crown help you guys make a decision?"

Sid and I laughed. I told the petty officer we used the truck's flatbed for a workbench. For us, it was a very handy tool. We got into the truck and drove away.

When we got back to our camp, I parked the truck close to our tent where I parked it most of the time. Sid and I told our guys the story about the navy petty officer's 7 Crown truck trade proposal. Some of the guys wanted to know how come we didn't take the offer; the 7 Crown addition to the deal might have made us a very nice, enjoyable evening.

The Condition Red sirens went off three times that night. When the light brigade got the bombers in their lights and the gunners let loose with the anti-aircraft fire, your sleeping time was over. Three times we had to jump into the air raid shelter. None of us slept too well that night.

In the morning, Ralph Clark was the first one out of the tent. I heard him say, "Alex, I thought you parked the truck close to the tent last night. Where's the truck?"

I ran out of the tent and looked where I was sure I parked the truck. The truck was not there. Somebody stole our truck, but how? We were up most of the night. If somebody had tried to start the truck, we would have heard it. The truck was loud when it ran. Somebody had to tow it away, maybe with some help.

I thought of the navy petty officer and wondered, could it have been him? As long as we were on Guadalcanal I never saw that old truck again.

Our small camp area was a few hundred feet north of Henderson Field and about a mile from the beach. To the west was the Lunga River, and a mile or so to the east was Tenaru River.

On the other side of the Lunga River, farther west, was Mount Austen, a very well fortified Japanese strongpoint. Farther west was Matanikau River.

Henderson Field was in the center of all operations and everything around, east, west, and south were battlefields.

Our field artilleries' constant bombardment told us the story of every offensive our Marines or soldiers were taking. We knew when our regiments went into action against the Japanese at Cruz Point. The Japanese put up severe resistance, and we had some heavy losses.

Damaged weapons were brought in for repairs from that battle. The men of the 164th Infantry Regiment told us the Japs were tough fighters, and they didn't know when to quit, but they said, "We'll get them on our next try."

We fixed their guns and wished them well.

Then we had some very good news.

Lieutenant Rabin said, "They're coming, they're going to be here today." He told us he received word that a group of our company men

8. Lieutenant Ben Rabin and Men Arrive

were on their way here, this time, bringing with them the machine shop truck, a bin truck with gun parts, a large 6x6 truck loaded with supplies and two small pickup trucks.

Apparently, our entire company couldn't come because the lack of space on the oceangoing landing craft, but they would come soon. They had to wait their turn.

Lieutenant Rabin, Sergeant DeBoni, and a few guys spent most of the morning at the beach waiting for the landing craft with our men. About mid-afternoon someone hollered, "Here they come!" Everybody dropped what they were doing and looked up. Our trucks, in convoy style, were slowly moving up the muddy road towards our small camp. They were our trucks, no doubt; each truck door had written on it in large letters, "22nd Ordnance Co. M.M." We helped direct the trucks off the road to our campground and park under the palm trees.

There was a reunion. With some hugs and handshakes, we welcomed our buddies to Guadalcanal.

Lieutenant Harold Witcolm and Sergeant Charles Mooney led the twenty man group. They were the most talented men in small arms and artillery repair, the help we needed most. The machine shop and gun parts they brought with them enabled us to give full support to the men using weapons in battle.

Lieutenant Rabin gave Sergeant DeBoni the task of directing the new men where to build their tents and dig their bomb shelters. To complete the job, they used the small pickup trucks to haul the logs needed for the shelters.

We tried to pick the best location for the machine shop and the bin truck. We parked them under the palm trees, hidden, not visible from the sky. Sergeant Mooney helped. Old soldier that he was, he always came up with the best suggestions for any problem.

I liked Sergeant Mooney. He taught me a lot about guns and military discipline. He had a philosophy about guns. To him, a gun was more than placing a bullet in its chamber and pulling the trigger. He compared a soldier and his gun to a musician and his violin. You must learn to play it to hear the music and take care of it, because some day your life might depend on it.

Within a few days the tents were built, the shelters were dug, the trucks were parked and the men were ready and eager to do their jobs. They didn't like the nightly air raids, but neither did we.

585 Raids and Counting

First and second group of 22nd Ordnance men on Guadalcanal. Back row, standing (left to right), first: Sergeant Laurence DeBoni, fifth: Sid Garrett, sixth: Jim Bertie, seventh: Alex Kunevicius, eleventh: Ralph Clark. Front row kneeling (left to right), first: Lieutenant Harold Witcolm, third: Joe Bargiel, eighth: John Burton, tenth: Louis Tennant, twelfth: Lieutenant Benjamin Rabin. Other men unidentified.

Now we had a machine shop, welding equipment, shop supplies, gun parts, and workbenches. We could fix anything in the weapons field that came our way. Very soon we acquired a name among the fighting battalions. We tried to fill their every firearms need, and they knew it.

Southwest of Henderson Field at Mount Austen, fighting intensified. The 132nd Infantry Regiment was preparing to attack the Japanese-held Gifu strongpoint. You had to cross the Lunga River to get to the foothills of Mount Austen. Getting supplies to them at times was very difficult, but we tried.

Jim Bertie was driving the pickup truck we called the weapons carrier. Sid Garrett was sitting in the middle, and I was sitting on the passenger side next to the door. We had just dropped off a load of weapons to an infantry company huddled at the foot of the hill. An ambulance was there picking up wounded men. When we started back, the ambulance drove

8. Lieutenant Ben Rabin and Men Arrive

behind us. The road was more of an old native path than a road. It was very clear area along the river.

As we drove along a small ravine, we heard the roaring sound of a plane and saw bullets strafing the road in front of us at the same time. If we were the target, the Japanese Zero fighter plane missed us by an inch! By instinct, Jim Bertie swerved the truck off the road down a small ravine. I must have hit the door handle with my arm. The door opened. I flew out of the truck and rolled down the hill. I rolled over a rock or a tree stump. I felt pain in my back. Maybe it was the shock. I wanted to get up and run. In seconds, Jim and Sid were next to me helping me off the ground.

The two ambulance drivers insisted I go in the ambulance to the first aid station. I told them I was okay. I didn't want to go, but they didn't listen. At the first aid station they unloaded the wounded men. In a little while, a doctor or a corpsman looked at my back.

He said, "You have a small bruise on your back. Go back to your camp and put some cold compresses where it hurts. You'll be just fine."

Jim and Sid were waiting for me. As we drove back to our camp, I was wondering, "Where am I going to get a cold compress? Maybe I'll call my mother."

By the time we got back to our camp I had a big welt on my back. When we told the guys what happened to us, the first sergeant wanted me to go on sick call for first aid again, but I refused to go.

He said, "If this welt was bleeding, I'd put you in for a Purple Heart." I'm sure he was kidding, but he told me to go lie down for a while and maybe soak a rag in cold water and put it on the welt. I did that, but he should have told me to put the soaked rag on my head because when I woke up my head was not clear. I was groggy. Rolling down that ravine I must have hit my head on something too.

This had to be one of my unlucky days, and if it wasn't for my good friend Jim Bertie, this could have been the worst day of my life.

After all the nightly air raids our guys became experts in how to react to almost every raid. The Condition Red sirens, the floodlights searching the sky for the incoming bombers, and the anti-aircraft guns firing shell after shell was the usual pattern. If you saw the bombers in the lights coming straight at your area, your best bet was to get into the air raid shelter and hope for the best. If the bomber released his bombs when you first saw him, the bombs would hit the ground when the bomber was right over your head. If you saw the bomber flying towards either side of you, you could stay outside the shelter and watch. You were pretty safe until the shrapnel from bursting antiaircraft shells fell to the ground. Again, you better get into the shelter, and if you heard the ripping sounds of bombs falling, it indicated they overshot your area and they would land some distance away.

The Japs became tricky in their air raid attacks. One of two bombers would fly in, get picked up in the lights, be shot at, drop its bombs and try to get away. At the same time another group of bombers would fly in from another direction, undetected, dropping their bombs at their will, sometimes at the floodlights or the antiaircraft guns. At times, our fighter planes, called "The Night Fighters," waited for the tricky Japs and played a trick on them! Shot them down!

When Condition Red sirens went off that night I managed to get out of my sack and stumble to the air raid shelter. Jim Bertie asked me how I felt.

He said, "Alex, why don't you sit on a sandbag next to the hole (the entrance). I'll watch."

Ralph and Sid were inside the air raid shelter looking for cigarettes. I sat down on a sandbag with my feet hanging down the entrance to the shelter. Jim was standing close looking at the sky. I remember looking up. The Jap bombers were caught in the lights. They were flying to one side of us, no problem, when the antiaircraft guns opened fire. We had time, at least that's what I thought.

Without warning, instantly with lightning speed, Jim Bertie dove into the air raid shelter and pulled me in head first on top of himself. I thought I heard a bomb exploding as I fell. The second bomb explosion rocked our shelter. The coconut logs supporting the top of our shelter moved. The sand and coral fell from all sides and covered us. I thought the shelter had caved.

Ralph hollered, "I think I have a broken arm!"

I was dazed.

It took us a little while to crawl out of the shelter, but all of us were okay. Ralph's arm was not broken. The stench of the sulfur and smoke filled the air. Our tent was lying on its side. Across the muddy road one of our small pickup trucks was on fire. Men with fire extinguishers were trying to put out the flames. Some men were walking around in a daze wanting to know what happened.

8. Lieutenant Ben Rabin and Men Arrive

Top: Alex Kunevicius, Joe Bargiel, and Ralph Clark standing in shelter, Guadalcanal, 1942. *Bottom:* Jim Bertie, Ralph Clark, and Joe Bargiel on air raid shelter near tent, Christmas, Guadalcanal, 1942.

585 Raids and Counting

At the beginning of the air raid a bomber snuck in from another direction undetected, dropped eight bombs, four in our camp area, but by some grace of luck there were no direct hits on any air raid shelters. The men were not hurt — shaken up, but not hurt.

About twenty-five feet from our air raid shelter the bomb left a good size crater. Our tent was caved to one side, full of shrapnel holes. Had I been caught sitting at the top of the air raid shelter's entrance when the bomb exploded, it would have been good-bye for me. Jim Bertie saved my life. We asked him what made him make that instant flying leap into the air raid shelter, pulling me into the shelter with him. He told us he really didn't know. He thought he saw a small flash in the distance, but he wasn't sure what it was.

He said, "Maybe it was nothing more than intuition."

Jim was a non-believer. I thanked him for pulling me into the air raid shelter and I also thanked the Good Lord for giving Jim the ability and good timing to make that flying leap.

All of us talked and wondered about what Jim really did see. Was that small flash of light he saw the very first microsecond of the explosion of the very first bomb the bomber dropped? Did that start Jim's intuition?

It was close to Christmas, so we decided to put up a Christmas tree. Since our tent was close to the road, everybody going by would see it. We took some palm tree branches and stuck them on top of our bomb shelter in an upright position. Since we had no Christmas ornaments, we tied a few hand grenades on the branches of our tree. Guys with cameras took pictures standing next to our Christmas tree. Some of the soldiers and Marines going by sang out to us, "Merry Christmas!" One such greeter surprised all of us. He almost staggered the mind.

The comedian, entertainer, actor, the very best of his time, Joe E. Brown, accompanied by another man, was walking towards us. He was dressed in army khaki. He had no hat or helmet. He had no weapon of any kind, and no military escort or guide. He looked as if he was walking down a street someplace in Hollywood. It was a wonder how he got here. How did a civilian get to Guadalcanal at this time and by what means and who would take a chance to bring him here? The battle for the island was going on full blast. Bombings, shellings, and strafings were a daily occurrence, sometimes by the hour, and here came a civilian through the jungle, the coconut grove, the bushes like nothing was happening.

8. Lieutenant Ben Rabin and Men Arrive

Alex Kunevicius decorating a palm branch, a would-be Christmas tree, Guadalcanal, December 1942.

Joe E. Brown and companion, Christmas 1942, Guadalcanal, on a visit to our camp.

When he saw us, I think he was glad. He stopped and talked to us. He joked around and we took pictures. Nobody asked him how he got here or why he came. In a little while he and his companion left us. They walked down the muddy road towards Henderson Field. They wanted to find the hospital.

Did he come on a ship or did someone fly him in? We never knew, but he made our Christmas a little bit better. Joe E. Brown, the famous comedian, was the only entertainer I ever saw while I was overseas. I never saw another singer, dancer, or comedian, ever; where I was, they were not.

9.

Christmas Day

Someone started a rumor about how we were going to have roast turkey on Christmas day. I thought it was Joe Bargiel. He knew everything and I believed him.

The 1st Marine Headquarters camp we built our camp next to was changing command. Army units were moving in with high ranking officers such as majors and colonels, and even an army chaplain.

On Christmas Eve the Japs couldn't resist lighting up the night by dropping bombs. They knew if they kept us awake Santa Claus wouldn't come.

Christmas morning at the headquarters camp, a Holy Mass was celebrated by Father Jim Dunford. The altar was set up on the hood of an army jeep. Father Dunford gave a general absolution to all the Catholic guys attending the Mass, and we all received Holy Communion. There were some non–Catholics there also. On Guadalcanal, praying was not out of style. Father Dunford gave a short sermon and wished us all a Merry Christmas.

Father Dunford became a great friend, a counsel, a fatherly figure to the men on the island. Everybody liked him. Christmas day we had turkey for dinner. That was a story in itself. We were the lucky ones. In the nearby hills, shelling went on all day. I wondered if the guys on the lines, the 7th Marines at Kokumbona, or the 164th Infantry at Cruz Point, or the 132nd Infantry Regiment at Mount Austen or the 2nd Marine Raiders had turkey that Christmas day? I wished they had.

Tokyo Rose became famous among the guys in the islands for the music she played: Glenn Miller, Tommy Dorsey, Benny Goodman. That evening she played Christmas carols.

From Tokyo on shortwave radio, she wished us a Merry Christmas, and said, "Wouldn't you rather be at home with your loved ones, holding your wife or girlfriend in your arms than lying in a dirty foxhole on Guadalcanal? American soldier, sailor, Marine, you don't want to die. Put down your arms, quit fighting. Emperor Hirohito is very good and kind. He will set you free to go home to your families. Why should you fight and risk your life for President Roosevelt? He doesn't care for you. Merry Christmas."

Tokyo Rose did play good music.

At the end of December we received a request from a 132nd Infantry commander who was fighting a never ending battle at Mount Austen. He wanted someone to make sure the Japanese 35mm small cannons found in the Mount Austen foothills after a battle were destroyed. The 35mm cannon used by the Japanese Army against our advancing infantry units fired shotgun type shells filled with pellets; they were very destructive. At times, the battle lines moved so fast the heavier gun positions were left intact. To make sure the guns left in such positions would not be used again, the commander wanted them destroyed.

Our artillery experts had a thermo-heat commanding grenade that looked like a small can of soup equipped with a fuse; when lit it had the power to burn through anything. But, to make the grenade work, you had to get next to the cannon, open the cannon's breech lock, pull the fuse pin out of the grenade, place it in the opened cannon's shell chamber and close the breech lock. When the grenade ignited, the heat was so intense that it fused the breech lock closed, never to be opened again.

Sergeant DeBoni, an artillery expert, was picked to command the dangerous job. He organized a small group of smart artillery guys to go with him: Frank Gornick, Eddy Kost, and Edgar Powell, all very knowledgeable in that field.

The army engineers were building a road from Lunga Point to the Mount Austen foothills. You were allowed to drive a small truck just so far. The grenades came in a wooden box that was not easy to carry. Sergeant DeBoni and his men drove partway, stopped, picked up their weapons and the box of grenades and walked to the Mount Austen foothills. Trying to find something in a wooded jungle area is like trying to find a needle in a haystack; everything looks the same.

The Japanese 35mm cannon is small, maybe 50 inches long, set on a tripod with two wheels and a hitch. On straight ground, one man can pull it with no problem, but on a hill among trees, it's hard to maneuver.

At one point, an infantry platoon sergeant showed Sergeant DeBoni

9. Christmas Day

Army engineers working on bridge across Lunga River, Guadalcanal.

two such cannons imbedded in a dug out trench and told him there was another one about 100 feet away, at the left side of the hill. The platoon sergeant told DeBoni there were snipers in the area: "Be careful."

Sergeant DeBoni and his crew wasted no time. They took care of the two cannons imbedded in the trench and headed for the other side of the hill.

Frank Gornick and the sergeant walked ahead, and Eddy Kost and Edgar Powell dropped back some, just in case. Eddy Kost carried a Thompson submachine gun. He was pretty good with it.

They walked pretty far, but they couldn't find the third cannon. Maybe they missed it, they thought. Frank spotted a small opening among the trees and something on the ground covered with branches. It was a wooden box. The sergeant and Frank removed the branches from the box, flipped the locks to the sides and opened the box.

The inside of the box was lined in dark reddish cloth. It contained a Japanese sword, several pairs of field glasses, a handgun, a small dagger, and a stack of letters tied with a ribbon. This had to belong to some high ranking Japanese officer, but why was it there?

Sergeant DeBoni and Frank Gornick didn't have much time to ponder why the box was there, because instantly all hell broke loose. Gunfire came from all directions. Both guys fell to the ground and buried their faces in the brush.

Frank Gornick said, "The gunfire seemed to come from the treetops with machine gunfire and everything stopped."

They lay there for a while longer and when they got up off the ground, Eddy Kost and Edgar Powell ran up to them and wanted to know what happened.

Sergeant DeBoni and Frank looked for the box. The box was gone.

Sergeant DeBoni said, "I was lying a foot away from the box during the gunfire. I never moved. Was the gun fire just a screen play to allow somebody to carry the box away? Was that possible?"

They heard someone holler, "What the hell you guys doing here? You want to get killed?" It was a Marine patrol watching that side of the hill. They told DeBoni the Japs were dug in all over the place. They popped up like rabbits. DeBoni tried to tell them about the box, a beautiful war trophy, but they didn't listen.

They gave the grenades to the Marines, told them how to use them and the four grenadiers walked back to where the engineers were building the road, got into their truck and drove back to camp. Thank God no one was hurt. The story about the box was told over and over again. Everybody had a theory why Sergeant DeBoni and Frank Gornick were not killed. I reasoned, to the Japs the contents of that box were more important than killing the two Americans. Speed was the answer. They got the box.

During the day, most of the time the activities at Henderson Field, planes taking off and landing and the roar of planes flying over the treetops, made it hard to hear yourself think. Every night the Japanese bombers kept everybody on the island awake and in their air raid shelters. Some of our men got malaria. Everybody had jungle rot. Some had it worse than others. I had it from my knees down. At night in my sleep I'd scratch down to blood. The medics issued blue ointment, Sulphathiazol, for the cure. The guys that had it on their neck and face looked like painted Indians, but the ointment didn't help.

After our entire company came and settled, our camp expanded in size and the demand for our services to the fighting units increased tenfold. The new M1 Garand semi-automatic rifle appeared on the scene and all

9. Christmas Day

the infantry companies wanted them in exchange for their old bolt action 1903 Springfield rifles.

The new rifles were issued as soon as we received them. The shipments we received were small, a hundred or two hundred rifles at a time. Some infantry commanders wanted immediate action and even tried the bribe method to be first.

One day I saw a Marine sergeant wink at Sergeant Mooney. That day we received 120 Marine-type, small, rolled up field mattresses; everybody in our company got one. They fit our bunks. They were nice. Sergeant Mooney made a good deal.

Our company commander, Captain Coyle, wanted to know why we received marine field mattresses but nobody knew why. Captain Coyle left it at that.

Was this another deal or just a small incident that happened to us on the other side of Henderson Field, that Lt. Rabin didn't want to be reminded of?

That morning Lt. Rabin told me to go get a jeep.

He said, "I have to deliver a package to a communication center somewhere on the other side of Henderson Field. I hope we can find the place."

The package he placed in the jeep was about four feet long, wrapped in a canvas cover, tied with rope. He didn't say what it was, but to me it looked like a couple of M1 rifles, maybe Jap rifles going someplace as souvenirs. The navy pilots landing on Henderson Field did a lot of horse trading.

The lieutenant asked me, "Were you ever on the other side of Henderson Field?"

I said, "Yes, sir, several times."

The length of Henderson Field's runway ran from the southwest to the northeast side of the island, about a mile long. Almost all of the Japanese nightly bombing raids ran the same way, from Tenaru Point to the Lunga River, the length of the runway.

Our camp was closer to the northeast end of the field. I was at that end a number of times, where all the activity was. The pilots' quarters and the guys that took care of the planes were there. That's where I was offered a better truck and a bottle of 7 Crown for that old flatbed truck we found in the jungle.

He said, "Alex, you drive."

I said, "Yes, sir," and without asking, I drove down the muddy road towards the northeast end of the airfield. While we circled the end of the field, several of our planes came in over our heads making a landing. Navy Seabees with their heavy equipment were all over the place, ready to fix anything the Japs tried to destroy with their artillery fire from up in the hills. We stopped once and the lieutenant asked the working Seabees for directions. About a quarter of a mile down the other side of the airfield we stopped at a tent with sandbags all around, shoulder high. It had a large antenna on top connected to a truck equipped with an electric generator. The truck was sandbagged on three sides. A few men standing around the truck were either guards or radio operators.

Lieutenant Rabin got out of the jeep, picked up the package and said, "Wait for me," and walked into the tent. He was there for a very short time, and when he came out he told me how vital and important this place was to the airfield's operations. It was the communication center between the pilots in the air and command post on the ground.

He got into the jeep and said, "Let's go back to camp."

I started turning the jeep around when the lieutenant stopped me.

He said, "Drive toward the end of the runway and the river. We can cross there."

I didn't like that idea at all. Between the end of the runway and the river, a path I drove once before to deliver some machine guns to the 25th Infantry Division fighting at a place they called Bloody Ridge, was not a good area to wander around in.

I said, "Lieutenant, I don't think the Seabees are going to let us cross the runway there."

He said, "Then we'll go around the riverbank."

We drove at the edge of the field until we got close to what looked like the end of the runway. Several men standing at one side of a large earth moving machine, as if hiding from somebody, were shouting and waving their arms, motioning us to stop. I couldn't hear what they were shouting, but I stopped the jeep.

They shouted again—loudly, "Get out of the jeep! A Jap sniper in the trees is firing this way! Get behind the jeep!"

I jumped out and crouched down behind the front tire and the jeep's hood. Lieutenant Rabin rolled out of this seat and scooted behind the jeep's rear end. There was a little bit of suspense, but not for long. Several loud bursts of gunfire from the ground and a Jap sniper fell to the ground.

Apparently, the Seabees reported the Jap sniper to the Marines long

9. Christmas Day

before we got there, and the Marines, when they got there, took care of the problem their way.

At the very end of the runway cut-down trees were being moved and stacked to make the runway longer. Two fighter planes came in for a landing. I knew we were in the wrong place at the wrong time. One of the men wanted to know what we were doing there.

He said, "Are you guys nuts? Get out of here!"

Lieutenant Rabin and I took the long way back to camp. After that the lieutenant and I spoke a number of times, but he never brought up the Henderson Field incident and neither did I.

The naval aviation men working at Henderson Field, the pilots and gunners and the men that took care of the planes, had no access to anything Japanese. Our camp was 100 feet from the airfield, and we dealt in guns of all sizes and shapes. We had a pile of Japanese rifles, automatic weapons, and machine guns gathered and brought here after every battle. We became a source for war trophies.

Navy pilots landing at Henderson Field to refuel took time out to

Men displaying large Japanese flag, considered a great trophy, Guadalcanal.

run over to our camp looking for something Japanese. Japanese handguns, small automatic weapons, and bayonets were all very popular. Sometimes a pilot would hand you a small bottle of liquor for helping him find something he wanted.

The most sought after and asked for war trophy was the Japanese samurai sword. We never had a Japanese sword brought to us, and I never saw one, but once I mentioned a sword to a young Marine and wound up listening to a fascinating story. He looked very young. He told me his name was Erick, he was from the state of Wisconsin, and he had to beg his parents to sign for him to join the Marines. He craved action. After his basic training he was placed in the 2nd Marine Raiders Battalion, commanded by Colonel Evans F. Carlson. Erick became a Carlson Raider.

Colonel Carlson became very famous for fighting in China on Nationalist Chinese leader Chiang-Kai-shek's side against the Communist leader, Mao Tse-Tung. He was an expert at guerrilla warfare. His battle cry was "gung ho" (work together). He led the 2nd Marine Raiders against the Japanese on Guadalcanal. According to the young Marine, they killed about 500 Japanese and lost very few of their own men. They came out of the hills to wait for their next assignment.

Erick asked me if he could trade his rifle in for something automatic, possibly a Thompson submachine gun or something with rapid fire, that would be more suitable for his kind of work. He told me Colonel Carlson didn't hold to battle line fighting tactics. He led his men with his guns blazing and shouts of "Gung ho" into Jap camps, killed as many of them as time permitted and retreated before the Japs had a chance to reorganize.

"Wow!" That was enough for me! I handed him a Thompson submachine gun and several clips of ammunition.

He couldn't thank me enough. He wanted to know if I'd like anything he had, a Jap gas mask, a water purifier, a small Japanese headband or a scarf? I listened to him for a while then asked him if he had a Japanese sword.

He said, "No," but he would go and get me one.

"Where are you going to get a sword?" I asked.

He said, "I'll go up to the hills. I'll get you a sword."

It dawned on me what the Marine was saying. He was going to go back to the hills, find a Jap with a sword, kill him and bring me a sword. He was either fearless or crazy. I told him I didn't want a sword, I didn't need a sword, I never wanted to see a sword.

9. Christmas Day

The young Marine smiled at me and said, "I know to the Japanese there is something very sacred about the samurai sword. They hand it down from generation to generation. Let me tell you how a real warrior, Colonel Carlson, reacted to a samurai sword."

He told me a few months ago in mid–August, somewhere in the Pacific, the 2nd Marine Raiders boarded two submarines and carried out the Makin Raid.

Makin, a very small island in the Gillbert Island Group, was occupied by a small Japanese force guarding a powerful radio station. The submarines arrived there at night. Erick was one of three men that volunteered to row ashore in a rubber raft to a designated spot on the island's shore. If they found the area unattended, as the commander anticipated, then with their navy flashlights they would make the prescribed signal for the entire force to land.

The three of them were told that if by chance they were caught, the surprise element would be gone, the raid would be cancelled and the submarines would leave. When they got into the rubber raft they each had a handgun, a bolo knife, a flashlight and a canteen of water. There were two sets of oars in the raft. There were no visible lights on the island. It was dark, but they could see the outline of the island against the sky.

The Marine asked me if I believed in angels.

I said, "Yes, I do."

He told me the wind and water currents were very strong and as hard as they rowed they missed their designated landing spot. He said, "Had we landed in the designated area we would have been wiped out. That part of the beach was guarded. My guardian angel was with us; we landed further down the beach and signaled to the submarines."

He told me how the Marines in rubber rafts landed on the beach with no problem, catching the Japs by surprise. They stayed on the island for two days, killed all the Japanese there and destroyed the radio station and the garrison.

Colonel Carson led the raid; he was always first, in front of everyone, unstoppable. President Roosevelt's son was there running around with two handguns blazing, like a western cowboy firing at everything that moved. The surprise raid was a success, and very few of our men were injured. We left the island in shambles.

As his men were returning to the submarine, Colonel Carlson was standing on the sub's catwalk watching them. One of the colonel's lieutenants getting out of the raft had in his possession a Japanese samurai sword. He walked up to the colonel and handed him the sword. The colonel held the sword up in his outstretched arms as if in tribute to a Roman war god, then placed the sword in a rubber raft and pushed the raft away. Everybody watched as the raft with the sword drifted away from the submarine. Everyone there who saw what happened knew Colonel Carlson was a warrior of warriors, and there was no other like him.

I saw the young Marine Raider just one more time. He asked me how we could stand being in the area we were in, with all those nightly air raids.

"Hard to live by; rather be up in the hills," he said.

I wondered if Erick ever made it home. I hope he did.

I got to know our ordnance colonel, Orrin Jacobson, pretty well. He often came around our work area and talked to us. He remembered me from the time Sergeant Horsley and I inspected the 2,000 rifles in some sort of dispute at a Nouméa warehouse. He was in control of all the new weapons shipped to the island. As soon as any new weapons came in, we issued them to the designated fighting units at his command.

We just finished issuing the last of a large shipment of new .50 caliber machine guns when Sergeant Horsley came in with a new assignment. He said, "Colonel Jacobson wants you to write up the working nomenclature of all the Japanese automatic weapons, machine guns, etc. Take them apart, describe the parts and how they work, and write it down."

"What the hell for?" I defended myself, "Why me?"

The sergeant said, "The guns and information will be shipped to Aberdeen Proving Ground, the Ordnance Center in Maryland — they need it."

I argued, "I can't write that up, I don't know what the parts are called. I'm not a writer. Why doesn't he ship the guns only? The ordnance guys in Aberdeen are smarter than me. They don't need any of my scribbling."

Sergeant Horsley said, "If you want, get a couple guys to help. Start now."

I lost the argument, but I also lucked out, and we got the gun project done in two days. Everybody helped.

We took each Japanese automatic weapon apart and spread the parts out on a workbench. The guys knowing how an automatic weapon works had no problem naming the parts and indicating what their function was. For each weapon to be shipped to Aberdeen, Maryland, we prepared a separate report, serial numbers and all.

9. Christmas Day

Some of the guns we listed were the machine guns, different in caliber, but similar in looks. They were well built and very easy to use. Each gun weighed about ten pounds.

The first type of machine gun, caliber 7.7mm, had a 30-round magazine that fed the gun from the top. The peep sight was set to the left of the magazine and did not interfere with sighting. The gun had a handgun trigger grip that was very easy to hold and fire. At the front end of the barrel the attached bipod was fixed to rotate from side to side. At the back of the gun was a wooden stock, and a handle on top of the gun's center balanced and made the gun easy to carry.

The next type of light machine gun looked almost identical to the first, but it was a 6.5mm with a 30-round magazine and a slightly shorter barrel.

The third type of light machine gun was made to be used from a vehicle. The gun was 6.5mm and hopper fed with a telescopic sight. It had a wooden stock connected to the trigger mechanism and a carrying handle.

Ralph Clark analyzing captured Japanese machine gun, Guadalcanal.

585 Raids and Counting

Since their guns were lightweight and somewhat scarce, they were sought after by pilots from Henderson Field as souvenirs. Most trades were good for a bottle of Seven Crown or a bottle of some sort of Australian whisky.

The 7mm heavy-duty machine guns were air cooled and set on large, heavy-duty tripods. Ammunition was fed from the left side of the gun by interconnectable stripper clips, 30 rounds each.

The most commonly used Japanese rifle on Guadalcanal was the long-arms Arisaka Type 99 7.7mm bolt action, with a 5-round clip and a place at the end of the barrel to affix a bayonet. The rifle was long and clumsy for jungle warfare.

Jim Bertie did most of the writing. He liked that. He kept track and wrote down the count of all air raids and shellings we encountered so far. His count was 62 bombings, 4 shellings and 5 strafings. In the company's orderly tent, Richard Dawdell typed the reports and made them look very professional.

The weapons we wrote reports on were put aside and prepared for shipment. Sergeant Horsley and Sergeant Mooney thought we did an excellent job. Before Sergeant Horsley turned the report over to Colonel Jacobson, he showed me the large brown envelope the report was in. On it was written,

> Aberdeen Ordnance Center
> Aberdeen, Maryland
> Japanese Automatic Weapons
> Nomenclature Report.
> Prepared by 22nd Ordnance Co. M.M.
> Guadalcanal, Jan. 1943.

When mail call was called, if you received a letter it was a very good day. A letter from home from your mother, father, wife or girlfriend was a blessing. Everybody had a different way of reading their letters. The guys that liked privacy walked away, read their letters, pondered about what they read, then read the letters again, and just sat there. Some guys read their letters out loud, sharing them with their friends, especially if there was something in the letter they liked, like "Hey, listen to this, Joanna really likes me. She said she loved me from the first time we met. She's going to wait for me to the end of time!"

Everybody loved those kind of letters. The guys' greatest fear, of those

9. Christmas Day

that had girlfriends back home, was to get the dreaded "Dear John" letter. My good buddy Ralph Clark got one of those from that beautiful girl he loved, whose picture he showed to everybody in our company. She wrote, "I've waited for you for so long, you're so far away. I don't know how to tell you this, Bill W. asked me to marry him, I said, 'Yes.'"

Ralph took it hard. He carried that letter in his pocket for a long time. Perhaps he thought the wording would change. I think all of us shed a tear in our hearts for our buddy Ralph Clark.

Most of the letters I received were from my mother. She wrote happy letters about my father and sister, about some of the people I knew, and even about her flower garden. She always ended her letters with a prayer for my health and a quick return home. Even sitting in a foxhole reading her letters gave me comfort.

One day I received a letter from her which was very different. She had a bad dream about me and seemed extremely worried. She dreamed my feet and legs were infected with blisters and sores, and I was trying to bandage them with rags. She wanted to bathe my legs in warm water and bandage them, but I kept running away from her and tried to hide.

Her dream had to be caused by telepathy. How else could she have sensed that there was something wrong with my legs? I had jungle rot very bad, from my knees down to my ankles. All of my buddies had it too; it was the curse of the island, and you scratched down to blood.

I answered her letter quickly. I wrote back and told her my legs were fine — I lied.

Sid Garrett received a package from home intended to arrive here for Christmas. It was way late but very welcome. He said it was a Christmas rum cake his mother made. She made one every Christmas when he was home. I had never heard of a rum cake; my mother made pies.

Sid took the rum cake out of the box and showed it to us. It was small and it had a small indentation in the center of the cake. He told us that's where you pour the rum. Out of the box he took out a very small bottle of rum, opened it and poured it over the cake. The rum soaked into the cake. It looked good, and we watched Sid cut the cake into five pieces.

I was so glad I was one of the five to get a piece of that rum cake. It was the best cake I ever ate. Maybe it was the taste of rum that made it so, or was it the island? I told the guys when I got home I'd buy a rum cake and a bottle of rum, pour the entire bottle of rum over the cake and sit there and eat it. Right then that was my ambition.

Sid Garrett said, "If I get home I'll ask my mother, maybe she'll bake you one!"

Captain Coyle, Lieutenant Rabin and the two sergeants, Horsley and Mooney, were coming towards the small arms bin truck. It had to be something out of the ordinary because we never saw them in a group like that before. Sergeant Horsley called the men in the small arms section to get together.

Captain Coyle said, "The new .50 caliber machine guns we issued to companies about a week ago don't work. None of them work. We're getting all of them back. We have to fix them."

The captain seemed very upset. He wanted to know if we did anything to the guns before they were issued. We assured him that all we did was take them out of the boxes and hand them out to the guys.

Captain Coyle said, "It's impossible that every gun issued doesn't work. Could it be the ammunition? Was there something new about the guns the gunners didn't know about? What could it be?"

What a peril and danger the gunners were put in: facing the enemy with guns that didn't work.

Later that same day, Sergeant Horsley told us why Captain Coyle was so upset. The news about the guns that didn't work somehow got to General Alexander Patch, the commander of the entire army task force on the island. Even before we received the first machine gun back at our workshop, the word was out that the guns were sabotaged by somebody at the gun factory back at home. General Patch was going to have the people at that factory investigated.

The men bringing the guns back pretty much had the same stories. The gunners tried to test fire the new machine guns, but they didn't work. The gunners tried to make adjustments, but nothing they tried worked.

Captain Coyle's order to the men was, "Find the problem and fix the guns."

Everyone in the small arms repair section became a gun doctor. The guns were taken apart, parts were changed, gun barrels were adjusted or changed. Everything seemed to be in order, but the guns didn't work. Had this been one gun that didn't work I'm sure we would have found the problem immediately, but according to the events, this was something big, desperately wrong, overblown, sabotaged, and that's why everyone looking for the problem knew they couldn't find the problem. Was this a curse, a Japanese curse? A .50 caliber machine gun fully assembled on an infantry

9. Christmas Day

type tripod was usually handled by two men. Our testing firing range was a tripod and an old bombed out shell hole, about three feet deep. The guys worked in pairs and took turns using the firing range.

My good friend James Bertie and I were working as partners and our tests were pretty much the same as everyone else's. A .50 caliber machine gun placed in a tripod in firing position has its sights on top of the gun's magazine. By pulling back the bolt handle on the right side of the gun you can lock the recoil spring in place, take off the trigger assembly and disassemble the rest of the parts.

Everything you usually work on is while the gun is in a face up position. There is only one part on the bottom of the gun's magazine, the breech lock cam, and the large screw holding the cam in place is wired, never to be touched by anyone. That we were told by a sergeant while still in training.

He said, "The cam is set and wired by the factory. Don't ever touch it, you big recruit."

Jim and I were going to test one more gun before the day was over. As we were picking up the gun to take it to the firing pit, my end of the gun slipped out of my hands and landed on its left side on the workbench. As I grabbed for the gun my eyes focused on the bottom of the gun's magazine and the brass breech lock cam. The flat screw with a flat head the size of a nickel holding the cam in place was wired but still allowed the cam some movement. Instantly, I put my fingers on the cam and tried to move it. It did not move.

I said, "Jim, the cam doesn't move. Let's cut the wire." We cut the wire and loosened the screw. The cam moved.

Jim said, "I think you found the problem."

We mounted the gun on the tripod at the firing pit, pushed the bullet belt through the chamber and pulled the bolt handle back and released it. The bolt picked up the bullet and placed it into the gun barrel. My heart was beating twice as fast as usual and Jim was hollering, "Press the trigger, press the trigger!"

I placed my hands on the handle grips and pressed on the trigger. The machine gun's rapid fire caused a dust storm in the shell hole. The rapid fire was heard throughout the camp.

Jim hollered again, "It's working, you did it, it's working!"

Within minutes everybody in camp was at the firing pit. Captain Coyle asked me to fire the gun again. I did, it fired, it worked.

The captain asked me, "What did you do to the gun?"

I told him, "I cut the breech lock cam's wire and loosened the holding screw."

Captain Coyle told Sergeant Horsley to have two more guns tested with cut and loosened breech lock cams. The guns were prepared and tested. They worked.

A glee came over the guys in camp as if we held onto a record, we never lost a game. It was as if we had just won a fabulous national baseball game and I had thrown a no-hitter against the opposing team.

The guys were asking questions. Jimmy Bertie was giving them the answers. Captain Coyle and Lieutenant Rabin said something to me, but I didn't hear them.

At that very moment I thought I saw my father standing there, smiling. He was my greatest inspirational advocate. He always told me I could accomplish anything, if I tried, and I certainly believed him.

There was a delay in going through the chow line that evening. It had never happened before. Our mess sergeant was standing at the head of the line next to a large pot with a measuring cup in his hand. He filled the guys' canteen cups as they walked by, and he was extremely generous with the stuff he was pouring with that measuring cup.

Someone asked, "What's that we're drinking? Grapefruit juice?"

There was a quick answer: "Yeah, spiked with torpedo juice."

Pure alcohol used to propel torpedoes dropped from airplanes aimed at enemy ships was nicknamed torpedo juice by the handlers. Sometimes it was used for other purposes, but nobody asked the sergeant how that stuff got into our grapefruit juice.

Everybody slept pretty well that night. If there were any air raids during the night, the guys in our tent and I missed them.

When Colonel Jacobson came to our work area that morning, he seemed to be in a very good mood.

He said, "You men did a fine job on those machine guns. I knew you'd find the problem. General Patch will be glad. He was worried."

To me he said, "I understand you're a pretty good chess player. Someday, I'd like to play a game."

I nodded my head in a "yes" gesture as he walked away. He talked to me at different times, and even called me by my first name, but this was a real surprise. How did he know I played chess? I hadn't played chess since I was drafted into the army, but I played chess. The high school I

9. Christmas Day

graduated from, the Father Jesuit Gymnasium, staged a monthly chess tournament for the students and some outsiders. I played in them and won some. To me, Colonel Jacobson never mentioned anything about a chess game ever again.

Tulagi, a small island north of Guadalcanal, about twenty miles across Iron Bottom Sound, was used by the Japanese as a seaplane base. The 1st Marine Division met with strong resistance from the Japanese when they landed on the island in August 1942.

Sometime later, an army unit replaced the 1st Marines, and the U.S. Navy used the island as a base for their personnel and vehicle landing craft. Our company received orders from General Headquarters to inspect all small arms equipment of the U.S. Army unit stations on Tulagi Island. I was one of the five men picked by Sergeant DeBoni to go to Tulagi Island to carry out the order. We were told it would be a two day job, to take our shaving equipment and a blanket. No need to carry any rations because we would eat with the troops there, but take some 6 chunk chocolate bars, just in case.

Early the next morning we packed our small pickup truck with our tools and gun parts and drove to the beach, to Lunga Point, where we were to meet a boat to take us there. There were no ships in the bay and very little activity on the beach. The bay's water was so still, its surface looked like glass. A single LCVP (Landing Craft, Vehicle, Personnel), beached, with its front end ramp down, was glittering in the morning sun. Several men were standing on the beach next to the craft. The craft's coxswain motioned for us to come.

Driving a truck on a sandy beach was tricky, but our truck was equipped with four wheel drive and we had chains on all wheels so we had no problem. Our disappointment was the landing craft's coxswain would not let us bring the truck on board. He told us there was transportation there waiting for us, and we should just bring up what we needed and leave the truck at the top of the beach. The landing craft's gunner threw each one of us a life jacket and told us to put it on. The craft's front end ramp went up and within minutes we were away from shore heading for Tulagi Island.

In addition to the craft's gunner and coxswain, there were three other sailors on board, going back to their units stationed on Tulagi. The coxswain informed us the trip would take about an hour.

So he said, "Enjoy the view and the ride."

585 Raids and Counting

From a distance Guadalcanal looked beautiful against the morning sky. We watched our planes flying overhead, coming in from patrols or raids to land at Henderson Field. We were about halfway to our destination. The bay's water was smooth, the breeze was pleasing, and we were enjoying the cruise. The craft's engine was very loud, it was difficult to carry on a conversation so the men were silent enjoying the view, daydreaming.

Without warning the craft buckled and the front end jumped up out of the water. Every one of us fell forward and then slid to the back of the craft and screamed. I was lying on my back against one of the men trying to right myself when I looked at the front of the craft. On the left side at the very front at the edge of the up and down ramp, there was a separation, a hole caused by something hitting us or our hitting something. As the craft settled downward taking on some water the coxswain gunned the engine full power. The front end rose and stayed out of the water.

I heard the coxswain scream at the top of his lungs, "Nobody move! Stay in the back." He was standing, holding on, steering the helm. Lying in the back of the craft in a huddle we couldn't see where we were or where we were going. Time was going by or standing still, I couldn't tell.

I think I finished repeating a dozen Hail Marys and maybe more when we heard the coxswain scream, "Hold on!" and the craft hit something and slid and all of us bounced to the front of the craft. The craft was lodged on a sandy beach.

"Thank God, we made it," someone hollered, and everyone repeated, "Yeah! Yeah! Yeah!" and there was other shouting coming from the beach. I looked. About a dozen or more young children, naked from top to bottom, were running toward the craft. A group of native men were standing farther up the beach waving their hands. They were wearing short pants.

"Where are we?" Someone asked, "Is this Tulagi?"

I didn't think the coxswain knew where we were, he seemed confused, exhausted, or maybe in shock, but whatever he was, he saved our lives. The gunner tried to lower the craft's ramp, but it didn't move. The children, three to ten years old, looked like they just came out of the water. They were climbing into the craft. The native men started walking towards us. They looked like the native men of Guadalcanal.

Each one of us carried a sidearm, a handgun, as we always did when we left our camp, but the native men looked friendly.

When they got closer one of our guys asked them, "What name this place?"

9. Christmas Day

They all shouted, "Savo, Savo, Savo."

We were on Savo, a very small island between Guadalcanal and Tulagi, north west, at the doorway to Iron Bottom Sound. There was no way we could fix the hole in the craft without proper tooling or heavy equipment. Looking at the damage everybody agreed we hit something, but what? Iron Bottom Sound was a graveyard for ships going down during the navy battles. I saw at least a dozen Japanese airplanes shot down over the bay; maybe they were still floating beneath the water. Someone suggested a baby submarine. Each one of us had a full canteen of water and several bars of chocolate. The sailors had some rations stored on the craft. Food wise, we were good for a few days.

We decided that at least one man would stay with the craft at all times and man the machine gun if need be while the others would go look over the island.

The natives were not exactly friendly, but they were cautious. Just a few months ago, November 12, 13, and 14, they witnessed one of the greatest battles in the Pacific, the Battle for Guadalcanal. We were there. I believe the natives were just leery of military people. At a nearby village, men with cameras were allowed to take pictures of the women and children. The women were covered from the waist down, but their breasts were bare. We gave the children some of our chocolate bars, and they brought us coconuts. The guys walked around the beach and all of us went swimming in the warm ocean water. This was like a mini-vacation for all of us, lying in the sand with nothing to do.

That night, we watched the Japanese bombers bomb Henderson Field. We could see the floodlights go up and hear our anti-aircraft guns and shells bursting in the air. I knew at that very moment, my buddies were there being bombed, huddled in their air raid shelters. I felt a little bit guilty for not being there. The mosquitoes enjoyed the new blood on the island; they were fierce! Nobody slept too well that night. Everybody was waiting for dawn. In the morning, the LCVP coxswain tried to convince us he knew where we were at all times.

He said, "When the collision occurred we were closer to Savo Island than to Tulagi." That's why he chose Savo Island. He told us a search party was already out to find us.

He said, "When an LCVP does not return to base after an assignment, a search order is issued immediately."

During the day a few planes flew over the island and one of them

Alex Kunevicius with natives on Savo Island, waiting to be rescued after unexplainable sea incident.

9. Christmas Day

even fluttered his wings. We had no radio communications but late afternoon we saw an LCVP coming our way. Our coxswain was right; the rescue crew found us. The four crewmen wanted to know what happened to us. It was a long story.

We transferred our tools and gun parts to the new LCVP. The sailors dismantled the machine gun and disabled the wrecked craft's engine. As we were leaving the island the men and children were waving goodbye. The guys threw their last chocolate bars to the kids.

In an hour or so we were back on Guadalcanal, and our truck was still there. When we got back to our camp, at first, nobody wanted to believe our shipwreck story. Everybody thought we just returned from our inspection tour on Tulagi. Sergeant DeBoni made his report to our company commander, Captain Coyle. The inspection was called off. We never had to go to Tulagi again.

A few weeks later, a story circulated the island that a Japanese baby two-man submarine washed up on one of the beaches with a wrecked entrance chute. I never saw the sub and didn't know if the story was true, but if true, could there have been a connection?

10.

A Hand Grenade That Flies

At Mount Austen the U.S. 132nd Infantry Regiment was having a difficult time trying to penetrate the Japanese stronghold. The Japanese soldiers on the hills, surrounded by large cliffs, dug in beneath the very roots of the trees, were almost impossible to get to. Shelling and aircraft bombing failed to crack their resistance. General Patch dispatched the 25th Infantry Division and the 35th Infantry Regiment to Mount Austen to bring to an end to the resistance and destroy the Japanese stronghold.

A lieutenant from one of the infantry regiments was trying to explain their problem to Sergeant Horsley. According to the lieutenant, the only remedy they had was to throw hand grenades into the caves, but they couldn't get that close to the caves or throw the grenades that far. What they needed was a hand grenade that flies. We in the small arms section listened in on the conversation. I believed our guys were best suited to solve any problem the infantrymen had, but how do you make a hand grenade fly?

The lieutenant said, "What we need is a slingshot or a way to shoot a grenade up the cliffs and into the caves."

A slingshot sounded like a good idea. The ancient Greeks and Romans used the over and under type slings using weights and pulleys, and it worked for them. And we had the advantage over the ancient warriors: we had rubber, so it should work for us too.

The conversation turned to how do you shoot a grenade up into the air, and off of what? Rifles was the word; we had rifles. One thought was to tie a grenade to the end of the rifle barrel and fire, but that was talked down because the bullet would pierce the grenade and it would explode. Taking the bullet out of the shell, using only the gunpowder, was a better idea. The best idea was to attach some sort of tube to the grenade, slip the tube over the rifle barrel, then fire the shell without the bullet.

10. A Hand Grenade That Flies

Sergeant Horsley thought it was a good idea. He took the lieutenant to talk to our company commander.

Within the hour, First Sergeant Russell Van Meter came to our work area and said, "Captain Coyle and Colonel Jacobson talked with the lieutenant about their hand grenade problem. The captain thinks we can help. He wants you guys to think about it. You know their problem."

Later that day, Sergeant Horsley brought in six hand grenades and laid them down on a workbench and said, "I know some of you guys can throw a grenade fifty feet or so. Big deal. I want you to think and find a way to deliver a grenade to a target 75 feet, 100 feet, or 150 feet or further with some accuracy."

He picked up a grenade and defused it by unscrewing the fuse assembly from the grenade itself.

He said, "This is a good way to start."

After the episode of the machine guns that didn't work, some of the guys kidded me that I had become Sergeant Horsley's golden boy when it came to some work assignments, but maybe it was because I had the knack of working on guns.

Sergeant Horsley looked at me and said, "Colonel Jacobson wants you involved in this project. Pick a couple of guys and see what you can do."

My pick was everyone in our small arms section, all my buddies. We knew we didn't have the luxury of time to sit and talk about it or draw diagrams looking for approval. We had to do something quick by trial and error.

All of us agreed that first we had to find a way to attach some sort of tube to a grenade and then slip the finished product over the end of a rifle barrel. After we removed the front sight from a 1903 Springfield Rifle we had 3½ inches of barrel space for a short tube.

Our cooks provided the empty soup cans, and our machine shop guys made up the 3½ inch tubes to fit over the rifle barrel.

Spot welding the tube to the grenade was the first thought, but we were afraid that might explode the grenade. By drilling four holes crisscross at the top of the tube and using the notches in the hand grenade it was easy to wire the tube to the grenade. Two days later we had three completed tube grenades lying on a workbench. They looked very simple, but making them was like grasping for straws every inch of the way.

Sergeant Horsley was pleased, and he announced testing time. We tied our sightless rifle to a tree at a 45 degree angle, slipped the tube with the grenade over the rifle's barrel, and placed a bulletless gun shell into the rifle's bullet chamber. To be safe, I tied a thin cord to the rifle's trigger and backed up behind a tree.

We had an audience crouched behind trees, everybody in the company, including the cooks, wanted to see the hand grenade fly. Standing behind a tree with the cord in my hand, I gave everybody watching a loud countdown, three, two, one, fire and pulled the cord! The shell fired, I watched the grenade fly up in the air about fifteen feet, spin and fall to the ground.

I thought I heard somebody laugh, and maybe the test was funny, but in my mind I knew the test was not a failure, it was a success. Almost instantly, we knew what the problem was. The 3½ inch tube was too short. The grenade attached to the short tube flipped off of the rifle's barrel before it could absorb all of the exploding shell's power. A short barrel handgun propels a bullet just so far compared to a long barrel rifle bullet that exceeds a distance of several thousand feet.

The machine shop men made up some eight-inch tubes. We stripped the rifle down to bare barrel to allow us the space needed and used the same procedure to make our test. Again, we had an audience. The gun was fired. This time nobody laughed. The grenade sailed and flipped through the air and landed about 75 feet away. Several more tests were made. We were getting better distance but we never could get any accuracy. All of our tests were done with disarmed grenades. We didn't know how a live grenade would have reacted using our rifle shot system.

Captain Coyle made a decision. Before any more tests were made on live flying grenades, he decided to send the men working on the project up to the hills to see for themselves what the fighting men really needed to get the Japs out of the caverns dug beneath the large trees.

Sergeant Horsley thought it was an excellent idea. He told us the frontline experience would do us good, make us better soldiers. The sergeant picked Ralph Clark, Sid Garrett and me to go with him to the foothills of Mount Austen where the Japs were putting up a very fierce battle against our infantry divisions.

When we got there we were met by a young lieutenant and a sergeant from the 35th Infantry Regiment that General Patch sent there to help finish the Japanese stronghold on Mount Austen. I'm sure the lieutenant knew we were coming because he was the same guy that came to our workshop looking for a way to get a grenade to a distant target.

10. A Hand Grenade That Flies

At the foot of the hill was a temporary first aid station with medics attending to the wounded men. Some men were sitting in the grass and in the brush eating or just resting. Some men were coming down and some men were going up the hill; the place was busy with activity. Higher up in the hills there was gunfire, and you could hear our artillery shells flying over our heads and exploding over the Japanese held positions.

The lieutenant said, "We're going to walk up this hill about five or six hundred feet. When we get to the large flat plateau we'll have to do some crawling 'til we get to the very edge of the embankment." Then he added, "You know, some of this area we took over this morning. Don't be concerned with what you see."

Sergeant Horsley made sure we had our helmets and handguns in place. I had my revolver hanging at my side, the .38 special I carried most of the time. The lieutenant started walking and motioned for us to follow. We walked through some wooded and high grass areas. I wondered how anyone could fight a war there. You couldn't see very far and in some places you couldn't see at all. When we got to the flat plateau the lieutenant told us about, we did some crawling to get to the embankment edge.

A small group of our soldiers was lying on the ground. Some had field phones in their hands. They were artillery spotters, a very dangerous job. They looked at us and probably wondered, "What are they doing here?"

Several hundred feet across a large ravine covered with very large trees in a jungle type setting, much higher than the plateau, we were lying at the edge of the embankment looking at the problem. From here, you just couldn't get there. In my opinion, if the Japs were dug in under those trees, flying grenades or no flying grenades, this was going to be a long and bloody battle place.

I thought, "If I were a general in charge, I'd surround the place and starve them out," but I wasn't the general.

The lieutenant and Sergeant Horsley talked for awhile and then the lieutenant motioned for us to follow him down the other side of the hill. There were dead Japanese soldiers lying in the brush.

The lieutenant said, "Those guys are there from last night's action. They'll be picked up soon."

I had seen dead Japanese soldiers before, but you never got used to the sight, and it's never a pleasure to see anyone dead.

A little bit further down the hill, Sid Garrett spotted him first. He said, "Look at that dead Jap! What is he holding in his right hand?" Everybody looked. In a little clearing a dead Jap soldier lying in the sun with his face up, his helmet and rifle to his side, was holding something in his hand over his chest that didn't look war related. Sid walked up to the soldier.

"It's a picture," he said, and he picked it up. All of us looked. It was a picture of a young woman. It had to be the soldier's wife or maybe even his mother. He was a young man. I felt a little twitch in my heart. This war was not a game. We were playing for keeps.

Sergeant Horsley looked at the picture for a while, looked at the dead soldier, and then slipped the woman's picture in the dead soldier's vest pocket. Nobody said a word. All of us walked down the hill.

The lieutenant said something about how he was going to check with us later about the flying grenades. Our visit with the infantry regiment was over.

On the way back to camp I was thinking about what a nice thing Sergeant Horsley did with that picture. That Jap soldier looked like a very young man. That picture had to be of someone he loved very much. He held it next to his heart when he died. He was going to have it with him forever.

Sergeant Horsley had feelings. He was a regular army soldier. It was the Greeks or the Romans or Alexander the Great that at times gave honor to the fallen enemy soldiers for their valor, their youth, their fierce fighting.

I liked Sergeant Horsley. He was a soldier's soldier.

A few days after our trip to Mount Austen we were told to abandon our work on the flying grenade. About a week later General Patch declared a victory at Mount Austen.

About two years later, one of our men, while back in the States at an ordnance warehouse, saw something he had never seen before. It was something on a tube with fins painted yellow. When he asked what it was, he was told it was a rifle grenade, something new. I wondered about that; could there have been a connection?

The 2nd Marine Division was relieved by the U.S. Army 147th Division to further the advance towards Tassafaronga Point along the coast line to Cape Esperance, a Japanese pick up and drop off point. The army engineers were building a pontoon bridge across the Matanikau River for men and trucks to cross with needed supplies for our advancing troops. We

10. A Hand Grenade That Flies

were told the bridge across the river was finished, and we could use it if we had to. A new supply of M1 rifles waiting to be delivered was loaded on a pickup truck. I was told where to take the rifles. I knew how to get there because I had been in that general area before. My companion, Larry Cox, and I knew to make our delivery we had to cross the river. It was a long drive. Within sight of the river, combat MPs stopped us and told us to wait until the engineers told us we could go across the bridge. A few trucks were there ahead of us waiting.

We asked the MPs if we could go to the river to see the bridge. The MPs told us on the other side of the river, Jap snipers tied in treetops were taking potshots at the engineers building the bridge. When our guys spotted them they sprayed the treetops with machine gun fire, but sometimes they didn't get them all. "Be careful!"

At the river, the army engineers were putting their finishing touches on the bridge. Some of the men were in the water, climbing up and down between the pontoon connections. They were wearing cut off fatigue pants and no shirts, and it looked like they were enjoying the water. The sun was hot, and it was about 100 degrees. The water looked very tempting.

On the other side of the river, we could see infantrymen spaced along the river protecting the engineers from any Japanese interference. At times there was rifle fire in the distance, but the engineers kept on working. A driver of one of the other trucks, also waiting to cross the bridge, opened a gallon can of fruit cocktail and asked us if we wanted some.

I said, "Yes, thank you," and pulled my canteen cup out and held it up. He filled Larry's cup first, then filled my canteen cup half full. The driver was hauling food supplies to the front lines. It was nice of him to share some of it with us. He was a nice guy.

I had never seen a military pontoon bridge being built before. Pontoons hooked together across running water with a road on top was a work of art. These guys were doing a spectacular job under fire. Larry and I were sipping our fruit cocktail, watching the show.

Larry nudged me with his elbow, pointed down our side of the river and said, "Look at the guy. What the hell is he carrying in his right hand? Is that a head or a skull?"

I looked. A soldier walking towards us along the river with his rifle and helmet hanging on his shoulder was holding on to something in his right hand that looked like a human skull, and the skull had hair. I didn't think the soldier saw us. He stopped, dropped his rifle and helmet on the

135

ground, got close to the water's edge and started dunking the skull in the water. He turned the skull sideways, tried to pour sand into the skull, shook it, and dunked it into the water again and again.

My appetite for the fruit cocktail left me instantly. I poured on the ground what was left in the cup. Some of the men sitting near us watching the soldier stood up.

Somebody hollered, "What are you doing down there?"

The soldier looked up and seemed surprised that somebody was watching him, that we were even there. He turned fast trying to hide the skull from us. He picked up his rifle and helmet and almost ran back down the river bank from where he came, carrying that thing, whatever it was. It did have black hair.

The army engineers finished working on the bridge and motioned to us; the trucks could cross. We drove across that new bridge, across the Matanikau River with no problem and made our delivery.

It wasn't very long after that day that the 161st Infantry and the 132nd Infantry linked up at Tenaro Point. The badly beaten Japanese were trying to evacuate their surviving troops at Esperance Cape. Most of the evacuating was done at night.

Even days later I couldn't forget what I saw at the bridge, at the river bank. I often wondered about the soldier and the skull. In his mind, did he believe what he had was a war trophy? Was that all it was?

It was the middle of February 1943 when General Patch proclaimed the organized Japanese army resistance on Guadalcanal was at an end. The last of the Japanese soldiers sick with everything the island had to offer died fighting or were evacuated.

Henderson Field was the busiest place on the island. Bombers and fighter planes were either landing or taking off by the minute. Troop transport ships were in the bay every day. Marine and army units were moving out, and new army units were coming in.

The nightly Japanese air raids never stopped. The big searchlights, the antiaircraft guns blasting and falling bombs was our way of life. According to my good friend Jim Bertie's count, from day one we survived 221 air raids and shellings. Jim wanted to go to college and become a math teacher. He could count.

Most of the air raids were one or two Jap planes coming in from different directions trying to confuse the antiaircraft gunners. Getting in and out of the air raid shelters once or twice a night became a ritual. The mos-

10. A Hand Grenade That Flies

quito attacks were fierce, but an Atabrine pill once a day kept the guys from getting malaria.

The dreaded body itch plaguing the men, jungle rot, was on its way out. The medics found sulphathiazol powder sprinkled on the infected, bleeding body parts cured the ungodly itch almost instantly. It worked a miracle for me.

Our company mess sergeant and cooks did their best to feed us with what they had. Everything we ate came out of a box or can. Spam prepared a hundred different ways and boxed mashed potatoes were on the chef's list every day.

Men talking about their mothers' cooking became a daily pastime. Everybody's mother was the best cook in the world. Some of the guys loved to eat. They claimed they lived to eat. I ate to live; food wasn't my life's priority. But I was absolutely sure that it was my mother who was the best cook in the world.

Father Jim Dunford, our division chaplain, came by one day accompanied by a protestant minister with some good news. He told us at division headquarters, just a few hundred feet away from our camp, the technicians were going to put up a screen and show movies. My first thought was maybe a movie with Betty Gable or Lana Turner, or some other beautiful girl with long legs. I expressed my joy about the coming event a little bit too loud, using the "F" word. Father Dunford heard me.

He said, "Young man, you used terrible language. I see you at Mass on Sundays. Maybe you'll come to confession first."

As a rule, I wasn't one for foul language. I didn't know how or why that word came out of me. I wanted to hide.

Soon after that I did go to confession. Father Dunford stood under a coconut tree and the guys walked up to him and confessed their sins to him face to face. I told him how much I liked girls, about Mira in Australia, and Jean, a married woman in New Caledonia. I thought Father Dunford was going to tell me I was going to go to hell, but he didn't. He told me to be sorry for my sins and that God is very forgiving. He gave me absolution and for my penance I had to say five Our Fathers and five Hail Marys.

After confession he whispered to me to stick around. As soon as he heard everyone's confession he was going to serve the guys some torpedo and grapefruit juice. I didn't know where he was getting the stuff, but it was good. I thought I would go to confession every time I saw Father Dunford under the coconut tree — who wouldn't?

585 Raids and Counting

The men in charge of the movie told the viewing audience that in case the Condition Red signal was blasted during showtime, use the few minutes to get to our air raid shelters. They would proceed with the movie after the raid.

I believe the very first movie shown at the Guadalcanal outdoor movie theater was a Laurel and Hardy comedy. General Patch was there, as were Captain Coyle and some of our officers.

Sitting on a coconut log was not exactly the Palace Theater, but feeling the ocean breeze under the open sky, nobody cared. Before the show, Father Dunford and his helpers passed out chewing gum and candy bars to the moviegoers. I received a candy bar. For me, a candy bar and a movie at the same time made it a very good evening. The air raid came after the show.

11.

Company Split Up

The army's favorite pastime, rumors, flowed like water through the camp. We had our share of them, some very good, like we're going to go to Australia for an extended leave, or we're going to go back to New Caledonia to take over our shop again. I liked that one very much, but Joe Bargiel, our king of rumor providers, had a rumor nobody wanted to hear. According to him, the 22nd Ordnance Company was going to be split up. A small cadre of men were going to leave to go somewhere to form another ordnance company. The main company was going to prepare itself for another island invasion. The next island up, northwest of here, was New Georgia, or maybe even farther up, Bougainville. That rumor nobody liked. It was amazing how many times Joe Bargiel's rumors were right on the money. That's why we called him king.

Within a few days a list of names was posted on a small bulletin board next to the company's office tent. Twenty men listed, two or three from each of our work sections, were going to leave the company. They were told they were going to go to Fiji Island and there become the cadre to form another ordnance company. My name was not on the list, and I didn't see any of my close buddies' names either. Three officers were on the list; one of them, Lieutenant Benjamin Rabin, was my favorite. I was sorry to see him go. There was a postscript: stand by lead time to departure, two hours. Not much time.

Reading the list and watching the men getting ready to leave the company wasn't easy. We were a close-knit company, together for two years. We were like family. Some of the men had a hard time seeing their very closest friends or good working partners leave. I knew I was going to miss my friends from my hometown in Ohio: Art Boessneck, Frank Gornik, Max Hange, Eddy Drozdz, and Bill Christopher. We always had something to talk about.

Two hours ran by lightning fast. The men filled one truck with their barracks bags and army gear and another truck was standing by ready to transport the men to the beach to board a waiting troop transport.

Captain Coyle was standing by, waiting for Sergeant VanMeter to get the men leaving in some kind of formation. The captain told them how proud he was to have had them under his command. He told them how good they were as ordnance men and he wished them well. He tried to say more, but he had a crack in his voice and I saw a few men wiping their eyes. Captain Coyle saluted the men and walked away.

There were handshakes and hugs and nice words spoken by all as the men climbed into the truck. We kept waving as the trucks rolled down the muddy road and disappeared behind the palm trees. A thought came to mind. I wondered if I would ever see any one of those guys again. Somebody had to have his finger on the timing button. It couldn't have been planned any better.

Our first sergeant dispatched a truck to the beach and it came back carrying two dozen men, young, new, just out of boot camp, just off the boat to join our company. They were in full army garb, with helmets on their heads and packs on their backs. They were sweating, standing there in the truck, holding on to their barracks bags. It was hot, at least a hundred degrees in the shade.

These guys were here to replace our buddies who had left us a few days ago. Amen. I sort of agreed with Sergeant Mooney's version of who the men were. They were "big recruits." I'm sure the new men weren't too happy with what they saw, looking down at us, stripped to the waist, with cut off short pants, no hats, yellow from taking Atabrine pills and tanned dark brown. I'm sure they wondered, "How did I get here?"

After a few days and some interviews with the company's officers and sergeants, the new men were assigned to different work sections. Three men were placed in the small arms section. One of our officers told us the new men would need some fast training.

He said, "Teach them all you know."

I liked Sergeant Mooney's idea better. He said, "We'll start them out cleaning that big pile of rifles We'll teach them what oil and a rag can do to an old beat up rifle."

We soon found out the new men had very little ordnance training, if any. One of the men, Jim Oak, told me he never even field stripped a rifle, so where did you start? All of us tried to teach them, and they tried

11. Company Split Up

to learn, but how do you teach someone all you know, what took you two years, handling vast amounts of army weapons, fixing everything that came by under all kinds of conditions? It would take time.

The big pile of beat up rifles was a good place to start.

My friend James Bertie had a philosophy that everything that happens has a reason. According to him, the world is created that way, such that when something happens here it affects something happening over there. I didn't have that much philosophy in high school, so I didn't want to argue against Jim's theory, but after that night I was almost convinced he was right.

It was a three Condition Red air raid night. The Japanese planes came in every few hours and the island rocked with gunfire. Even the mosquitoes with their full bellies tried hard to hide in the air raid shelters.

In the coconut grove at our camp the parrots were everywhere. They had their nests in the palm trees and they were a nuisance at night with their laughter. They sounded almost human. We were told to leave them alone. They were beautiful but full of bugs. That night the parrots outdid themselves. They tried to outdo the bombs and the gunfire with their laughter. It was as if they were in some large theater, hysterically laughing at some comedian's jokes, all night, without stopping, loud.

"Those parrots are telling us something," Jimmy said, as he jumped into the air raid shelter. Early that morning I told Jim he was absolutely right about an action bringing in a reaction. It brought me a sleepless night. Jim grunted in disgust at my remark.

The company hadn't been called out in formation since sometime in New Caledonia. When the whistle blew and the First Sergeant VanMeter called the company to formation, the guys were in disbelief. Everybody wanted to know, "What happened?" When our company commander, Captain Coyle, walked to the front of the formation Sergeant VanMeter called the men to attention and then told them to stand at ease and said, "Captain Coyle, now Major William Coyle, is leaving the 22nd Ordnance Company and wants to say goodbye.

Everybody said, "What? What did he say?"

James Bertie was standing right behind me and kicked me in the back of my shins. I knew why. Major Coyle started to say something about how proud he was to be the commander of such a highly qualified group of men, but he didn't finish the sentence. He walked a little closer to the formation and tried to say something again, but nothing came out. He choked up.

585 Raids and Counting

The men broke formation and encircled the commander and reached for his hand. He was a good man, a fair man, an excellent company commander, and the guys liked him. He was the only commander we ever had and he had that fatherly touch.

Some of the men saying goodbye had tears in their eyes, and he, the tall Texan that he was, shook their hands and wiped the tears from his eyes.

Later that day we drove Major Coyle to Henderson Field. We were told he was going back to the States to take charge of a new ordnance depot.

The parrots were extremely quiet that night.

One of the biggest and most damaging Japanese air raids on Guadalcanal, Henderson Field and the ships in the bay occurred on April 7, 1943. Early in the morning over 175 Japanese bombers and fighter planes attacked the island. The U.S. Navy destroyer *Aaron Ward* was sunk and a number of transport ships suffered severe damage. Five or six of our fighter planes were shot down.

The Japanese bombers concentrated their attack on Henderson Field. Our fighter planes engaged the Japanese bombers and fighter planes, some at treetop level. Bombs, shrapnel and bullets came from all directions covering the ground. Our antiaircraft guns fired round after round without stopping. Everybody ran for cover.

The Japanese bombers came in groups then broke up into different bombing patterns. Their fighter planes tried to fight off our fighter planes going after the bombers. A good number of Jap planes were shot down and dropped into the bay.

Henderson Field was warned of the air raid and cleared of planes beforehand, but the runway and some of the airfield's structures were severely damaged and burning. Navy Seabees with their heavy earth moving equipment were on the runway minutes after the raid, filling in the bombed out craters. Our camp, a stone's throw from the airfield, suffered some damage to our vehicles and tents, but by some miracle none of our men were hurt.

In our workshop, I turned my head to see who was talking to me. A young soldier with piercing eyes, standing at parade rest and holding onto a rifle almost as tall as he was, said, "They told me you can fix my rifle." I looked again. The rifle the soldier was holding onto was between 5 and 6 feet long. I had never seen a rifle that big.

11. Company Split Up

I said, "Where did you get this thing? What is it? How do you shoot it? What's wrong with it?"

He said, "It's a Springfield .50 caliber rifle. I shoot at Japs hiding behind trees. I'm a sharpshooter."

The soldier was by himself. He had a little giggle in his voice. He looked out of place. He had to belong to some unit somewhere.

I said, "What's wrong with your rifle?"

The soldier told me that when he sighted in a target and was ready to fire, the trigger pull was too hard, and sometimes it caused him to miss the target.

He said, "I'd like a softer trigger pull, maybe a hair trigger, can you do that?"

I said, "I can try," and reached for the rifle. It weighed at least 15 pounds. There was no way anyone could fire that rifle in an upright, standing, or kneeling position, and if fired correctly, the .50 caliber bullet recoil would surely break your shoulder. I was sure you had to rest that gun on something to make it work, without killing the shooter.

We did have a tool to check the trigger pull of any gun, but I had never used it. I used my trigger finger to determine the right pull of any gun. I was always on the money. It was a very common request by men wearing handguns, revolvers and pistols to ask for a softer trigger pull. I fixed many of them. They were easy to do.

That .50 caliber rifle looked exactly like the 1903 Springfield .30 caliber rifle, only it was almost twice the size. I laid it down on the workbench, made sure it was unloaded, closed the bolt and pulled the trigger. In my opinion the trigger pull on this rifle was way beyond the 2 pounds prescribed for the .30 caliber rifle and other guns. First I oiled the moving parts and tried it again, but it was pretty much the same. This rifle needed more help.

I disassembled the rifle's bolt and oil stoned the part that catches the firing pin to the trigger part called the sear. The holding space between the two parts was about 1/16 of an inch. I oil stoned the sear. By stoning those parts at different angles you could bring that space down to almost nothing, creating a hair trigger. When I finished, I put the parts together, oiled the stoned parts, closed the bolt and pulled the trigger. It was perfect. I tried it again. For me, the trigger pull for this rifle was better than perfect. I knew the soldier would like it. He was watching me. I opened and closed the bolt again and motioned for him to try it.

Max Hange and Alex Kunevicius at the grave of General Tojo's son, killed on Guadalcanal, 1942.

He moved the rifle forward and leaned over the workbench almost in a lying position. It took him a little time, but then he pulled the trigger. I heard him say, "My God, could it be?" and then he recocked the rifle again. He pulled the trigger and this time he jumped up and out loud said, "It's perfect, it's perfect. How did you do that?" He kept thanking me, and I kept telling him, "It's okay, it's okay."

Before he left he said, "The sergeant told me your name, but I forgot. What's your name?"

I said, "My name is Alex."

He said, "Alex, every time I fire this rifle at a Jap, I'm going to mention your name. He'll know why he went to hell."

Sergeant Horsley and I watched that soldier walk away carrying that .50 caliber rifle. Sergeant Horsley said, "I told that soldier to see you because in all my 20 years in the army, I never saw a gun like that."

As the soldier disappeared in the jungle, I wondered if the devil were to ask the Jap shot with the big gun by what means he got there, would the Jap mention my name?

11. Company Split Up

At the end of May, we received a new company commander, Captain Paul Conti, and two second lieutenants. One of them, a lanky, thin fellow looked like he had just come out of boot camp, a 90 day wonder. His name was Tripp. The second guy came wearing an Australian pith helmet and short pants. He looked more Australian than a U.S. Army officer. I could never remember his name because he wasn't with us very long.

A few times I saw him walking through the camp, holding his left arm behind his back, looking at the ground as if he had lost something. One night he woke up the camp, shouting and firing a Thompson submachine gun at the moon.

The moon over Guadalcanal was very bright; you could read a book at midnight with no problem. Maybe it was just too bright for him.

The next morning the lieutenant in Australian garb was gone. We never saw him again and nobody cared. We were too busy with other things. New troop movement on the island and landing craft in the bay indicated something big was in the works. According to the information we had Admiral Halsey issued orders to invade New Georgia, the next main island in the Solomon Island Group. Munda Airfield on that island was the big prize.

Large Japanese air raids during daylight hours increased to staggering numbers. U.S. fighter planes stationed at Henderson Field intercepted Jap bombers and fighter planes coming in from Bougainville and some as far as Rabaul. The battles were fierce. The Japs always lost more planes but kept coming back.

Our work and gun inspections increased by tenfold. Many of the troops were issued the new M1 Garand rifle. The semiautomatic gas operating M1 rifle was so different from the old 1903 Springfield rifle the troops had before that the soldiers had many questions. Many of our inspection trips were instructional.

At the end of June we received news that the 4th Marine Raiders landed at Segi Point in New Georgia and the Army 43rd Division landed on the island of Rendova, about 10 miles across the channel from Munda Airfield on New Georgia, the real target. Army and Marine divisions were leaving Guadalcanal heading north covered by darkness. At times, we knew which division was leaving: the 25th, the 37th, the 169th. We had close contact with all the divisions while they were on the island.

During this very active period First Sergeant VanMeter passed the word to the men that the company was put on moving alert. The 22nd Ordnance Company had to prepare for another island invasion.

An order was issued to the designated drivers to put chains on all truck tires, front and rear. All of our trucks were equipped with front wheel drive, to make them safer to drive on sandy beaches. Sergeant John Ankeny, in charge of all automotive activity, told me he was going to send two of his men to help me put chains on the

Top: Bin truck with gun parts parked under tent flap for camouflage, Guadalcanal, 1942. *Bottom:* Ordnance bin truck stored with gun parts and tools, used as a repair shop and hidden in the jungle, Guadalcanal.

11. Company Split Up

bin truck I drove. John was from Ohio and a good friend of mine. I thanked him.

This was the time we had to be ready to move in an instant and still do our work. Our trucks gave us the big advantage. They were gassed at all times. We were able to break camp, load everything in our trucks in a few hours and be on our way. Each truck had a designated driver and an assistant driver. I drove the bin truck that looked like a school bus. My assistant driver was James Bertie. We were ready, and we waited.

Daily news, rumors and stories were coming in from all directions. Joe Bargiel and our barber, Forrest Lentz, were competing for first place for who had the most accurate story about our next venture.

Forrest had his barber shop set up right next to his air raid shelter.

Ordnance bin truck, Guadalcanal.

He was a very cautious guy, but he knew what was going on in the company. He cut our new company commander's hair. Forrest had the advantage and he talked. But this time, both guys were betting our next venture would be the island of New Georgia, and almost all the guys agreed.

Even in a very stressful time, we found something to laugh about. Eddy Drozdz was a commercial artist. He could accurately draw a picture of your face in a few minutes. Some of the guys had Eddy paint their girl's picture from a photograph they carried in their wallet. His painting always looked better than the photograph.

Somewhere Eddy got a piece of plywood 2½ feet wide and 6 feet long and painted a life size beautiful girl, our company sweetheart. The girl was naked, standing sideways with a flower in her hair, her butt sticking out, with long legs and high heeled shoes. She was holding a sign that read, "22nd Ordnance Co. Hdqs." The guys named the girl Miss AnnaBell. Everybody loved her. She was fixed to stand in front of our orderly tent, and some guys even saluted her as they walked by.

General Patch's two adjutants, a colonel and a lieutenant, were scheduled to come visit our company headquarters. Our new company commander, Captain Conti, became concerned about AnnaBell standing in front of the orderly tent when the adjutants arrived. He thought it would be better to cover her with a tarp. Somebody had a better idea. A hula skirt was made out of

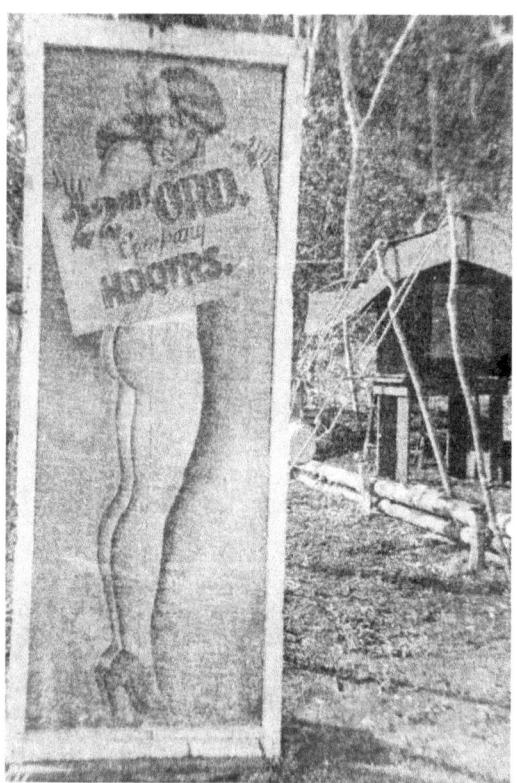

AnnaBell. The Ordnance boys loved her. Drawn by Edward Drozdz.

11. Company Split Up

palm tree leaves and pinned around AnnaBell's waist. She looked ravishing.

When the two adjutants arrived, the other guy, the colonel, took a great interest in AnnaBell. He kept looking at her. He stood next to her to have his picture taken. He touched her hula skirt 'til it fell to the ground. The colonel leaned over to pick up the hula shirt and when his face was in a very inappropriate position, the lieutenant took his picture, and when the colonel stood up holding the hula skirt in his hand, the lieutenant took another picture.

According to First Sergeant VanMeter, everybody standing in that group watching the colonel laughed. The lieutenant laughed out loud and handed the camera to the colonel. The colonel opened the camera, took out the film, handed the camera back to the lieutenant and also laughed. It turned out to be like a scene from a funny movie. All of our men enjoyed the story and laughed. AnnaBell never had to wear the hula skirt again.

12.

Sasavele Island First, Then New Georgia

The month of July went by and we were still waiting for our orders to move. The men were ready, the trucks were gassed up and had chains on all wheels to drive better on sandy beaches, and our work equipment was partially torn down and packed.

The reports coming in from the island of New Georgia varied in optimism. Marines and army units advancing toward Munda Airfield encountered fierce resistance from the Japanese Army. Japanese positions at Munda Field were constantly bombarded by U.S. planes from Henderson Field, and most of our information about the fighting on New Georgia came from the guys manning those planes. In some cases, food and supplies were air dropped to our fighting forces in thick New Georgia jungles. The Japanese soldiers were hard to beat fighters.

On July 15, in an enormous air battle, our planes shot down 45 Japanese bombers and fighter planes. On July 25, our Navy destroyers shelled Japanese positions near Munda Field. At the very beginning of August, our troops battled their way forward destroying Japanese units on Bibilo Hill and finally taking Munda Field.

On August 5, General Griswold announced that Munda Field was in U.S. hands. On the night of August 6–7, three Japanese destroyers carrying troops to New Georgia were sunk by our Navy torpedoes.

The army's 25th Infantry Division under General J. L. Collins landed on New Georgia and pressed the enemy north. Because we were so close to the field, we were on constant Condition Red air raid alert.

In the second week of August, one morning the whistle blew and the company was called to formation. Our company commander, Captain Conti, told the men that the company had received orders to move. The

12. Sasavele Island First, Then New Georgia

entire company, men, trucks, and all equipment, would board a double deck landing craft this evening. Our landing time would be tomorrow morning on the island of New Georgia. All men would wear their helmets and carry a firearm. His message was short but very clear.

When the captain walked away from the formation, Sergeant VanMeter told the men to take down their tents, clear the work areas and pack everything in the trucks. We would have one more meal there before we left.

Then he shouted, "Break camp now. That's an order!"

We took down our tents and cleared the work areas. The portable workbenches and tools we packed and strapped down in the bin trucks. When everything was down, the only thing left standing was the tent flap that covered our latrine. It was still being used.

The designated truck drivers were given their spot in the truck lineup. The bin truck I was driving was marked number six to come off the landing craft. The company cooks outdid themselves that day. Everything they had opened or not tied down in the truck was put out as a feast. It was our last supper on Guadalcanal.

We were very familiar with the beach at Lunga Point. We picked up most of our supplies there. The beach was sandy but not hard to drive on. When we got to the beach, the double deck landing craft (LCIT) was there waiting for us. It was evening.

The large 6×6 trucks were the first to back up the ramp into the landing craft, then the bin trucks, then the small trucks and jeeps. I had no problem backing into my parking spot. The corpsman directing traffic did a fine job. When all the trucks were in place, the corpsmen told the drivers to put the truck transmission in gear and pull the brakes on as tightly as possible.

The men gathered on the upper deck. We were the only company there. Immediately the landing craft pulled up its ramp and pulled away from the beach, made a large semicircle in the bay and then headed northwest. It was getting dark, but you could see the silhouette of the island. I wondered if I would ever see Guadalcanal again.

The landing craft engines were loud, but the men were very quiet. There was no smoking on the upper deck. Bertie, Clark, and I found a good place to sit at the very end of the craft. It was dark, but you could see the churning wake the craft was making. If you looked at the wake long enough it would put you to sleep.

Landing craft ready to move the 22nd Ordnance Company to New Georgia, August 1943.

I heard men snoring. When I woke up, the moon was halfway up the sky, climbing to the stars. The guys always said, "The Solomon Island moon was the largest moon in the world." At times it looked so big you could almost reach it. By its light you could read a book or write a letter or see a Jap hiding behind a tree looking your way.

I heard someone say, "This is not good. I could see a mile."

In the moonlight, the craft was leaving a wake a mile long that looked like a white highway. We were in open waters. The concern was that if we could see that far, somebody unfriendly could see us too. By watching the wake we could see the craft was zigzagging, and above the craft's loud engines we could hear aircraft flying above us. We were in submarine alley. Japanese subs looking for our troop ships and U.S. PT boats looking for Japanese navy destroyers made these inter-island waters extremely dangerous.

I never heard the 120 men I lived with for all those months as quiet as they were that night. I think all of them were praying. I know I was. I almost wished my mother was there. At home she led the family, my father, sister, and me, in prayer. I really missed her.

12. Sasavele Island First, Then New Georgia

At early morning, just before dawn, we were sailing along some small islands. The landing craft seemed to be sailing at faster speed, it wasn't zigzagging anymore and there wasn't aircraft activity overhead.

And then it was dawn. There were islands on both sides of the craft and it was now traveling at full speed towards what looked like the biggest island in the area. There were no ships or craft of any kind to be seen anywhere. It looked like we were alone, but not for long. Two Jap planes chased by several U.S. fighter planes flew over our craft and dropped their bombs but missed by a hundred feet. Another Jap plane followed our planes over the craft and also missed by several hundred feet. The machine gun fire by our fighter planes was deafening.

We were about a thousand yards from what looked like the big island when the landing craft made a sudden sharp turn and at full speed headed in another direction. Someone on a loudspeaker kept repeating, "Drivers, man your trucks." Bombs fell again, this time close enough to make the craft rock. The Japs weren't giving up. There were other landing crafts in the area that we didn't see before. We were not alone.

The men gathered on the lower deck were ready to disembark as soon as the ramp was dropped. I was sitting in the bin truck holding onto the steering wheel when I saw the craft's corpsman run to the ramp and pull something. There was a loud scraping noise then a sudden stop, and the ramp fell to the ground. Men fell, I hit my head on the steering wheel, and Jim Bertie sitting next to me fell against the windshield. When I looked up I could see the beach and trees, the inner jungle about a hundred feet away. The men ran down the ramp on the beach and disappeared into the jungle. The corpsman was waving the first trucks off the craft. They were driving towards jungle looking for a place to hide under the trees. Then it was my turn.

I learned to drive very young. I had a car and a driver's license before I was drafted and I never had an accident. Maybe that's why they made me a designated driver. I was a good driver. In seconds, I drove the bin truck down the ramp onto the sandy beach. I could feel the wheels dig into the sand. One of our sergeants pointed for me to go to the right. Trusting the front and rear wheel drive and the chains on all wheels, I swerved the truck to the right, drove along the beach, and looked for an opening in the jungle. Down the beach, I saw a light spot between the trees that might have been an opening. Jim Bertie, sitting in the passenger seat saw it at the same time and hollered, "Go there! Go there!"

Banyan tree on Sasavele Island, August 1943. Some were so large you could drive a truck between the roots.

12. Sasavele Island First, Then New Georgia

Our planes were overhead protecting our landing from the Jap bombers. I could see them flying along the beach. I turned the truck to the left and drove it into the opening. It looked like somebody used the opening for a walking trail. I drove about 100 feet into the jungle and stopped the truck between two enormous buttress roots against the tree. The buttress roots were at least eight feet high, a very good shield for the truck. I later found out it was a banyan tree that only grows in the tropics. Other trucks followed us and filled the opened trail. Most of the trucks were under cover. Soon the landing craft that brought us here disappeared, and there were no planes overhead. It was quiet for awhile.

The men gathered in groups, and all of them had the same comments: "This place is crawling with crocodiles!" and "Where in hell are we?"

I saw one of those crocodiles. It was a black lizard about six feet long, and it ran from me.

The sergeant managed to get the men together again. Captain Conti told the men that apparently something must have happened to our pre-arranged landing place on the island of New Georgia. We were now on a very small island named Sasavele, just a stone's throw away.

He said, "If you look to the left side of the big island, you could see the outline of Munda Airfield. That's where we were supposed to land." Then he added, "We should be off this place in a day or two."

We had fish for dinner that evening. At one end of the island, about 100 feet away, was another tiny island, or a part of Sasavele, separated by ocean water waist deep. You could see the sandy bottom and schools of many fish. We had a few guys who claimed to be great fishermen. Several hand grenades, an army net hammock with ropes at both ends, and the company cooks with portable grills provided the evening meal. It was much better than eating Spam and chewing on a piece of coconut.

During the night we watched the Japs bomb Munda Airfield. A small amount of antiaircraft fire indicated the U.S. troops were in control of the field. Most of the guys slept in trucks, or in hammocks off the ground because of the lizards.

The next morning we boarded the same landing craft (LCIT) and with no fanfare landed on the island of New Georgia, at one end of Munda Airfield, in heavy beach sand and coral. We were directed from the beach, across a road, up a small hill onto a field the size of a ballpark with no trees, no bushes, or even a blade of grass. The place looked like the Sahara Desert, only it was all coral.

585 Raids and Counting

Munda Airfield, New Georgia Island. All coral, no shade and very hot.

We circled our trucks like the pioneers in the prairie with their wagons, ready to defend themselves against the Indians. This area had to be intended to park airplanes, but the general probably changed his mind and gave the place to us. I couldn't believe this was the place we were going to build our camp, but we did. We put up our tents, dug the air raid shelters in the hard coral, and set up our workplace. Almost immediately men from all directions brought in weapons with problems.

I didn't know how they found us so fast. A few truckloads of battle scarred weapons dumped on hard coral put us in business again; we did what we did best—fixed guns.

On slightly higher ground, a few hundred feet away from our camp, an antiaircraft battery group was sandbagging their floodlights and gun positions. Wow! Having them for a neighbor was a blast!

As soon as Condition Red sirens sounded, telling the island that Jap bombers were coming, the gunners turned on the floodlight generators, and they were loud. When the floodlights went on searching for the Jap planes, they lit up our entire camp for the Japs to see. We had no cover. When the guns opened fire, our entire camp shook and it was almost

12. Sasavele Island First, Then New Georgia

impossible to tell the gunfire from bombs bursting. We were just too close to the action. This was a once or twice a night occurrence, night after night after night.

We soon learned we had another kind of problem, not so severe, but always at night. We couldn't take our shoes off when we lay down to sleep. In the morning we found the shoe invaders snuggled inside the shoes, the land crabs. It was hard to shake them out of the shoes. At certain times of the month the land crabs came out of their holes and went to the ocean, not hundreds, but thousands! If you walked at night, you stepped from one crab to another. To get to the ocean, the crabs had to cross the road. Trucks using the road at night smashed the crabs against the white coral. In the morning when the sun came out and cooked the smashed crabs, the stench was horrifying. Crabs weighed from one to two pounds. We weighed one mama crab in at 26 pounds! They were no good to eat.

13.

Kolambangara

The Japanese troops still left on New Georgia were trying to find their way to the next island, Kolambangara, while the U.S. forces wanted to stop or destroy them. Our artillery men helped to set up long range artillery guns on the northwest coast of New Georgia to shell the Jap positions on Kolambangara. Sometime at the end of September to the beginning of October, the Japanese realized they couldn't hold onto Kolambangara and evacuated the island.

When Lieutenant Charles Tripp called out six names, I wondered why he called mine. He and I had very little to do with each other, and I didn't think he liked me. He had nothing to do with the small arms section, and I didn't exactly like him either. He came from North Carolina and I think he thought the boys from Ohio with names like mine were below his dignity.

He told us that the next morning a small military task force was going to invade Kolambangara. Headquarters believed most of the Japs were gone from the island. We had been ordered to send a few ordnance men with them just in case they needed us. We were to wear battle gear, and we would leave at 4 A.M. LCT traveling time was to be 3 hours.

When we boarded the LCT that morning, the combat team, about 200 men, was already there. They were quiet. The LCT backed off the beach and for a short time headed northwest, then turned north and after an hour entered a water passage between two islands, New Georgia on the right and Arundel on the left.

At dawn we could see a landing craft about a mile in front of us and one about a mile behind us. I looked at the sky. It was very clear, and I wondered how soon we would have company we didn't want, but there was nothing up there but birds. If it wasn't for the landing craft's engines, it would have been very quiet. I had noticed this before: men are very

13. Kolambangara

quiet before an invasion. Most of them think of their loved ones or say a little prayer. When we entered Kula Gulf, between New Georgia and Kolambangara, our planes appeared in the sky; they were fighter planes patrolling Kula Gulf.

Kolambangara, about thirty miles in diameter, is a volcanic island northwest of New Georgia. As we approached the island, we saw other landing crafts landing troops there ahead of us, and as we got closer we heard loud shouts and cheers like you hear at a football game. There was no gunfire and no Jap planes in the sky, a very good reason to cheer. Our craft hit the beach and the men disembarked in a few minutes. We followed, and everybody walked to the mountain. The place looked like somebody lived around there for a long time. The trees were trimmed, there were paths to walk on and the front of the mountain had an entrance to a cave beautifully carved, fit for a king. This had to be the general's quarters. Nearby, a wooden porch-like structure covered with canvas had to be a place to rest for the officers.

Electric generators, wiring, hand crank Victrolas and American records were scattered on the ground, Benny Goodman, Guy Lombardo, Glenn Miller, etc.

The Japs must have left this mountainside in a hurry. The ground was covered with trash. Thousands of little white envelopes marked Sweet Skin were all over the area. I picked one up and looked inside. It was a condom. Why they needed condoms on this rock was beyond me. One of our bombs must have hit their supply source. I put one in my pocket to show it to my buddies.

The landing craft left the island. We were told the first men getting off the landing crafts and cheering were either Australians or New Zealanders. They disappeared into the jungle. I didn't get to see them. The troops we came with were in the area searching for something. I saw one of them carrying a Victrola and some records. Some of the men were picking up the little white envelopes off the ground. An officer and a few men were trying to find a way to haul away an electric generator. I thought that was dumb.

Our little group and Lieutenant Tripp stayed together. We found a gun position and some beat up Japanese machine guns and rifles, some with bayonets fixed. We walked along the beach and checked a few other gun positions. Some of the bigger guns were lying in the sand, disabled. All of us wondered what we were supposed to do there, if anything, and why did we go there?

Japanese fortified cannon emplacement, bombed out by U.S. bombers on Kolombangara Island, 1944.

Toward the evening we walked back to the beach at the landing place. We slept in hammocks that night and in the morning the landing craft came back to pick us up. It soon filled with troops, backed off the Kolambangara beach and headed for New Georgia.

Lieutenant Tripp didn't say very much during this entire ordeal, but just before we landed back at New Georgia, he tapped me on my shoulder and told me he knew I spoke several different languages.

I said, "Yes, sir."

He asked me which ones.

I told him I spoke Lithuanian, some German, a little bit of Polish, and I understood some Russian. I also had a few years of Latin in high school.

He said, "You know, there is a request by the war department to offer men with more than one language to go to Europe. They'll send you home for a two-week furlough, give you some training, and you'll go to Europe. Are you interested?"

I said, "No, sir. I'm not interested."

He said, "Think about it. They may even offer you a commission."

13. Kolambangara

I was a bit surprised the lieutenant mentioned Europe to me and how he knew I spoke more than one language. I was even amazed he spoke to me at all. I was sure he didn't forget what happened between us back on Guadalcanal.

All of us knew about a young fellow called Jamok. He was transferred to our company from some infantry regiment. Supposedly, he was pinned down behind some logs and branches in a gun battle with the Japs for hours after his regiment pulled back. He fought his way out of that battle but became a very nervous young man. He was very good at handling a Browning automatic rifle. Several times he accompanied us as a gun cover guy while we were on a detail looking to find and destroy small Japanese cannons left behind after a battle.

Jamok was always trying to help me carry or lift something while working, and he called me Sarge. That morning, Jamok ran into the bin truck where I was looking for some parts, and with great excitement and almost out of breath, "Sarge, in the storage tent across the road, guys are stacking fixed rifles on the ground. I told them that's wrong, but they didn't listen. Go see, they'll listen to you!"

I said, "Jamok, what are you talking about? Who's doing what?"

He repeated, "Guys are stacking rifles on the wet ground. That's what. Go look!"

Both of us walked across the muddy road to the storage tent where the rifles were stored. Since we were short of rifle boxes, most of the time we used coconut logs to stack our fixed rifles on.

When we entered the tent, two guys I knew were rearranging some boxes and one guy with no shirt on, our very new lieutenant, was telling them what to do. Jamok pointed his finger at a stack of rifles four or five feet high stacked from the ground up. No logs, no support of any kind, right on the ground. The tent was about ten feet from the muddy road, with water all over the place. The ground was always wet.

I saw the lieutenant but my first words to the guys working there were, "Hey, you guys! You can't stack those rifles on the ground! You know better than that!"

I was going to tell them to get some logs, but before I finished my sentence the lieutenant in a loud voice belted out, "Who are you? What's your name? I'm Lieutenant Tripp. I give orders here!"

Also in a loud voice I said, "Lieutenant, unless you get those rifles off the ground right now I'll have to report this to our company commander."

585 Raids and Counting

This time he turned blue, and hollered again, "What's your name? What are you doing here? I'll have you court-martialed," and he ran out of the tent.

Jamok looked at me and said, "Do you want me to shoot him in the foot?"

I said, "No, I don't want you to shoot him at all!"

Jamok and I walked back to our shop work area, and I told my buddies what happened to me with that new lieutenant. My buddies thought it was funny.

In a little while we saw First Sergeant VanMeter and Sergeant Mooney walking across the muddy road to the storage tent. They stayed there a very short time and walked back to the orderly tent. About an hour later both sergeants came to our work area and called me aside.

The first sergeant said, "Lieutenant Tripp is very upset at how you spoke to him in the storage tent. I told the captain about the guns on the ground. I think the captain is going to give the lieutenant a desk job in the orderly tent."

I grinned.

Sergeant Mooney said, "The guys are going to pick up the rifles and restack them on logs. The big recruits should have known better."

I never heard another word about the incident. Lieutenant Tripp never crossed my path or talked to me until the day when I was one in a group picked to go to Kalambangara.

When we arrived back on New Georgia and disembarked, Lieutenant Tripp never again mentioned Europe to me.

That night I played some poker with the guys. I had a queen high straight flush dealt to me in a five-dollar limit game. How many times does that happen in a lifetime? I made a bet, nobody called.

Instead, maybe I should have thought a little more about the languages and the War Department's offer. I wondered if they played poker in Europe.

The tropical sun on New Georgia cooked not only the land crabs but it cooked everybody and everything that moved. We were only a few hundred miles from the equator. The sun's rays coming straight down penetrated our tents, our trucks, our work areas. Getting into our parts trucks to work was like getting into a perpetual sauna. By noon the temperature reached 100 or 120 degrees, and only at night did the strong trade winds give us some relief.

13. Kolambangara

The real remedy came to New Georgia with wind, rain, lightning, and thunder. We were told to prepare for a hurricane. It was early for the season, but it was coming.

The first hurricane we experienced in New Caledonia was when the French garrison commander offered our company commander safe cover for us behind the fort's stone walls, but our company commander refused the offer. In two days our camp was destroyed.

Planes from Munda Airfield left the island. Planes in need of repair were staked and tied down. All shipping to the island stopped, and the harbor was empty. We learned from our first hurricane experience that the pyramidal tents are the first to come down. For us, there was no place to hide. It was sit in a truck for a few days or hide in the air raid shelter.

The wind and rain intensified, and the war on New Georgia stopped. The ocean waves flooded the beach and came over the road and up the incline towards our camp. During the day the men were trying to keep their tents up by any means possible. More rope and more tent stakes in the ground helped some. Everybody was soaking wet, but some of the tents were still standing.

The worst part of the storm came during the night. From higher ground, where the anti-aircraft gun positions were, rivers of water came through our camp, and washed away anything not tied down, down to the beach. Air raid shelters were full of water. Some of the trucks were in a foot of water, but still standing. The running water carved ditches in the ground. You had to watch where you walked.

After being wet and cold for two days, watching the sun come out from behind the clouds made life worth living again. The company cooks made hot coffee that morning. I didn't know where they got the water. Maybe it was rain water, but it was the best coffee I ever had in all my life.

The Navy's Seabees were out there first with their equipment fixing the water damaged airfield's runway, and very soon our planes started coming back from wherever they were.

The ocean calmed down and a few craft appeared in the bay. It took us about a week to rebuild our camp, but everybody suffered some personal losses. Letters from home, pictures of loved ones, anything of importance kept in barracks bags either floated away or got mixed with muddy coral, and then the war and the bombings started all over again.

Sergeant Horsley introduced the man to the guys in our small arms

585 Raids and Counting

Navy Seabees working on Munda runway, New Georgia Island.

repair section as an Australian coast watcher. When I looked up, he looked more like a man who just got out of the jungle. His big hat was folded to one side. He was wearing short pants and a khaki shirt with no military markings. He had a long holster hanging from a leather belt studded with large caliber bullets all around, like a western cowboy. The revolver inside that holster had to have an eight inch barrel or longer. He wasn't a big man, but he looked like he could take care of any giant, maybe even Goliath!

Sergeant Horsley said, "I want you guys to meet Mr. A.R. Evans. He's a coast watcher, a real friend to the U.S. military, and a real hero."

The sergeant explained Mr. Evans' activities as a coast watcher and what it meant. He lived in the jungles with the natives, spotted Japanese ship movements and signaled the information to the U.S. forces — a very dangerous job.

Sergeant Horsley said, "Just last August, about the time we were landing here on New Georgia, Mr. Evans helped rescue the crewmen from the U.S. PT Boat 109 the Japanese destroyer rammed and split it in half, near the islands Olasama and Naru. He and his native friends swam out to the hurt crewmen, helped them swim to the shore and gave them first aid."

13. Kolambangara

As we listened to the story, Mr. Evans standing there looked very modest, but he had a little smile on his face.

Sergeant Horsley said, "Mr. Evans has a little Belgian pistol that needs some work. Alex, maybe you can take care of it."

Mr. Evans handed me the little pistol and said, "This little pin and spring came out of it someplace, but I can't take it apart. It doesn't work."

The pistol was small. It fit in the palm of my hand. I never saw one like that before. First I removed the magazine from the pistol. It was full of bullets. Mr. Evans, the sergeant, and my work buddies were watching me. It took me several minutes, but I took the pistol apart and found the place the spring and firing pin went.

Somebody took this little pistol apart and left the spring and firing pin out. The part that held the firing pin in place was there. I replaced the spring and firing pin and locked it in place and reassembled the pistol. Mr. Evans watched me assemble and wipe clean the pistol.

He asked, "Will it work?"

I placed the very small bullet magazine into place, cocked the pistol and fired a shot into a sandbag. It worked.

Mr. Evans was very thankful. He patted me on my back, asked me to come to Australia after the war, and walked away with Sergeant Horsley.

In 1961 or 1962, I was at home watching the evening news. An Australian gentleman was being honored by President John Kennedy in Washington, D.C., for saving his life in August 1943 in the Solomon Islands, when a Japanese destroyer rammed P.T. Boat 109, which Kennedy commanded. I recognized the man. His name was A.R. Evans.

14.

New Caledonia Again

Rumors and talk of rumors about leaving New Georgia were all over our camp. The men reasoned because we were in the Solomon Islands almost two years and our camp sites were next the airfields, we endured every raid the Japs threw at us.

According to Jim Bertie's shelling and air raid count, we were now at 585 raids and counting, so we must be going some place to take a rest. Joe Bargiel, the rumor king, was in his glory and John Burton, the company bookie, was giving odds to where we were going to the guys willing to bet. Some of the sergeants hinted the rumors about leaving were true but didn't know the destination. Our company skeptics, the known crepe hangers, speculated our next stop would be up north, Bougainville, another invasion under fire. I was praying against that one.

Most rumors died in a few days, but this one hung on and got even better. Everybody wanted to believe we were going to go to Australia or New Zealand or back to our old campsite and shop in Nouméa, New Caledonia.

When the official order to move came from the company commander, it was New Caledonia.

Some of the guys grumbled. They were wishing for Australia or New Zealand, but I was very pleased because I knew my way around Nouméa very well. About ten days later our troop transport pulled into Nouméa Harbor. We helped the merchant marines unload our trucks and in convoy form drove through the streets of Nouméa, by the French fort, to our old campsite. The French soldiers standing at the fort's gate waved to us as if welcoming us home. Below the French fort, our campsite overlooking the most beautiful part of the bay had not changed. By evening, our tents were up, the trucks were parked, the kitchen was in working order, and the cooks managed to have chow ready for the hungry guys.

14. New Caledonia Again

If I were a general, I would have given the guys an A for their efficiency. Our guys were the best at everything they did. I was lucky to be one of the group. My thoughts were that I too played a part in this great ordnance company, and that night everybody slept all night.

It took us a little bit longer to get the old workshop in working order again. Whoever occupied the facility while we were gone made it into a messy junkyard. Wooden boxes, pallets, and broken wheel carts were stacked several feet high. A half dozen native men were hired to haul the stuff away and clean up the area. When we got the shop in working order again, we soon found out the work needs and priorities in New Caledonia had changed. There were no more inspection trips up the island. Most of the soldiers and Marines enjoying the streets of Nouméa were men who had seen action somewhere and were here to take a rest. Sailors here off the ships waiting for repairs spent their time in small bars or looking at girls. The beverage store shelves were filled with bottles of wine and beer. The small restaurants were doing a bang up business, and everything was double in price. For us, this was a big surprise. There was a USO in the middle of town with young girls pouring coffee and passing out magazines. What a difference two years made.

At night, Nouméa was lit up like a Christmas tree; no fear of a Jap bombing attack anymore. In the evenings we were free to go to town, from camp, a twenty minute walk to any part of Nouméa. We were issued some new khaki clothes and we looked like soldiers again.

About the third week after we returned, I decided to go see Jean Poulier. When I came to her house I wondered if she would be glad to see me again. I felt a little bit of joy. I really wanted to see her.

I walked up to the window with the shudder, where Jean first handed me a bottle of wine a few years ago and knocked.

I heard a little girl's voice call, "Mama, Mama!"

The window shutter swung open. It was Jean. She looked at me. She looked stunned. She grabbed her face with her hands, and kept staring at me.

In a very quiet French tone, she kept repeating my name, "Alex, Alex, Alex, you are back."

She stretched out her arms for me to come in and wrapped her arms around my neck and held on. I held her tight for awhile, 'til her little daughter, Jeanine, got in between us and gave me a hug.

Jean asked me to sit at the table, and in a little while she brought in a bottle of wine and some bread and cheese. We talked mostly about where I was, how lucky I was to come back unhurt, and how I missed her, and she missed me, and how glad she was to see me again.

We drank the wine and sat there looking at each other, but I sensed there was something about her that was different. She was struggling with her English.

She said, "Alex, I want to tell you something."

I said, "Tell me what?"

She said, "I think you no come back. I think I no see you again. I cry for you."

I reached out, took her hand, and said, "But I'm back."

Gently she pulled her hand away from me and said, "Alex, I tell you about my husband, him coming back to Caledonia, him free."

I must have made a funny face or some sad expression because she stopped talking and watched me for a while. In French and in her best English, she told me she received a letter from her husband from New Hebrides where he was confined by the U.S. Army for being a Vichy French officer. He was released and now he was a Free Frenchman. He wanted to take her and little Jeanine to Australia and start a new life. He loved her and Jeanine very much.

She said, "Alex, I want to believe him. I must give him one more chance."

I felt a little twitch in my heart, but I had no claims on her, two years had passed, and I was sure I was going to leave her again. Maybe this was best for her and little Jeanine.

I gave both of them a hug, walked to the door, turned and looked back. Jean looked beautiful. She was crying and wiping her tears. I wanted to go back and hold her, but I didn't.

She lifted her arm and in a very soft voice said, "Ta, ta, Alex, ta."

I struggled to say, "Goodbye, Jean," and walked out of the house.

After that, I was in town a number of times, but I never saw Jean Paulier ever again.

It was the first Sunday in October 1944, a day I'll always remember. My churchgoing buddies and I attended the 10 A.M. Holy Mass at St. Joseph's Cathedral in Nouméa. U.S. soldiers, sailors, and Marines filled the church. Most of my prayers were prayers of thanksgiving for letting me survive two years in the Solomon Islands. I felt if I kept thanking God for everything up front, He would be too embarrassed to do me wrong. It worked for me for some time.

14. New Caledonia Again

When we got back from church, we saw something happening in camp, unusual for a Sunday morning. Men standing in groups, some in shorts, waving their arms as if discussing something very important, and some men were running towards the orderly tent. The camp was jumping with action. I figured there was something wrong. Good God, I must have said the wrong prayers this morning at the cathedral.

Somebody shouted, "Go look at the bulletin board! We're going back to the U.S."

I jumped out of the truck and ran towards the orderly tent. The bulletin board was surrounded by half of the guys in the company. I tried to read the note pinned to the board.

It read, "Men leaving for the United States," and some dates.

I missed the rest and went down the list and read the names "James Bertie, Joseph Bargiel, Sid Garrett, etc."

I scanned down to the K's on the list. What a disappointment.

There were about fifteen men on the list going back to the U.S. The word was all original 22nd Ordnance Company men would be rotated back to the U.S. as soon as replacements arrived. Everybody wondered how the first names on the list were determined; perhaps the alphabet had something to do with it.

Later we were told the company commander and the first sergeant pulled the men's names at random from the company roster. The men would get to go home on a two week leave and then be assigned to some army post, most likely as ordnance instructors.

For me, saying goodbye to Jim Bertie and Joe Bargiel was pretty hard. They were my best buddies. Both of them said the same thing: "Alex, we'll see you in Cleveland."

One week later another list was posted with fifteen men going stateside, but my name wasn't on it either. New replacements flooded the company. They looked like they just got off the boat, with no ordnance training.

The first sergeant told us, "Teach them all you know, and do it fast."

Sergeant Mooney asked me if I ever flew in a pontoon airplane.

I said, "No."

He told me there was an order to do an ordnance weapons inspection on a small island outpost, about two hundred miles from us.

He said, "They're going to fly a couple of you guys in there to inspect their weapons. It's a small outfit. You'll be back the same day."

The next day Sergeant Mooney told me there was a change in plans. The water around the island was supposed to be too rough for the airplane to land. We were going to go there in a yard boat.

I asked him, "What's a yard boat?"

Sergeant Mooney came back with a smart answer. He said, "It's the boat that patrols the yard."

I liked Charlie Mooney. He had a sense of humor.

That evening three of us from the small arms section and Sergeant Mooney boarded the yard boat. The boat looked like a yacht, at least sixty feet long, painted dark gray. The half dozen young men on board were not U.S. sailors. They spoke with an Australian accent. This was an Australian boat, and it flew an Australian flag. The captain of the boat told us it would take about ten hours to get to our destination.

He said that if we had no problems, on the way back we would stop at a French speaking Polynesian island that we'd never forget. He said that we'd have stories to tell our children. It was called Lifou Island.

The captain told us we were free to go anywhere on the boat, only no smoking on deck after dark. We could help ourselves to coffee and boxed rations that we would find in the small galley.

I figured this would be one beautiful cruise for us, and it was, all but for one unfortunate thing: the beep. As soon as we were out of Nouméa Bay, the beeper started to beep. The beep was loud, about four seconds long, a ten second delay, and then another beep. I timed it. It was four beeps per minute all night. It never stopped. The beeper was a depth finder located below the main deck, attended by a sailor, sitting next to it, wearing earphones.

I didn't sleep a wink that night. I didn't think anybody did. Towards morning, the air was chilly, and the hot coffee was a blessing.

At dawn, we approached Melfa Island. It was small, a dot in the ocean. The captain directed the boat into a small inlet cove, sheltered by a rock barrier against the big waves. Now I could see why a pontoon plane would have a hard time landing in the rough waters. The captain sailed the boat next to a wooden pier with no problem. He must have been here before.

We were met by a lieutenant and a sergeant, and in less than five minutes they drove us to their camp. About a half dozen pyramidal tents with their sides open were scattered about in a very tropical setting.

Some of the men were walking around the camp with very little on.

14. New Caledonia Again

To me, this place looked like a summer resort for some very lucky soldiers. At a supply tent, we field gauged about 75 rifles, several .50 caliber machine guns, a couple B.A.R.'s and a few .45 caliber pistols. All of the weapons were clean, well oiled, and in good working condition. On top of the hill, the highest part of the island, this little army outfit had the best four .50 caliber machine gun stronghold emplacements I ever saw. Over the treetops, the guns were in very good condition.

I thought, "When Sergeant Mooney writes his report, I'm sure he will give this army unit, 'Excellent for weapons care.'"

In my opinion, this inspection trip was well worth the effort.

The lieutenant invited us to have lunch with them, and the cooks went out of their way to prepare a tasty meal for us. We had grilled Spam, some fish, and something to drink that had a little zing to it. Nobody asked them what it was.

The yard boat captain told us it would take about four hours to get to the island he told us about.

He said, "If you like the place, we will spend the night there."

As we traveled, we could see small islands on one or the other side of the boat. The beeper was on. To me, it seemed the water was always smoother when we were out the farthest from any land. At one point, the captain pointed out a shark close to the yard boat. The shark looked very light, almost white, about fifteen feet long. He traveled along side of the yard boat and then disappeared. It was late afternoon when the yard boat headed straight towards an island, over some rough water, over a reef into a mile long horseshoe bay with palm and banana trees, a village of small grass huts and children running along the beach and swimming out to meet us. I thought I saw paradise. The captain dropped anchor about 100 yards from shore and the sailors dropped a dingy into the water.

The captain said, "This is the island of Lifou. The people on this island are Polynesian, they are very friendly, and they speak French. They are Catholic. You'll see why when you get there."

We got in the motorized dinghy, the four of us and two sailors, and propelled our way towards shore with children swimming out to meet us and cheering us on. The dinghy slid onto the beach. All of us jumped out and I looked up. A dozen men in short pants but no shirts were standing nearby looking at us and waving their hands. At the village edge women standing in groups, wearing dresses, some holding babies, were just looking. They were Polynesians, olive skinned, good-looking people.

On a small cliff just above the beach was a small church with a big wooden cross dominating the view. A tall man standing near the church wearing a black cassock and a pith helmet was waving his hands in a greeting gesture. He was an older man. He had a short beard and a big smile on his face. He was the missionary priest.

The dinghy went back to the boat to pick up the other sailors. We walked through the village and tried to talk to the people. A woman handed me a banana, and a little boy standing next to her held his hand out waiting to be paid. I pulled out a dime and a nickel and held them in my hand. The boy took the nickel. It was bigger than the dime. The children followed us like in a parade. The teenage girls standing next to their mothers were beautiful. The guys couldn't keep their eyes off of them. I had the same problem. I was more than willing to spend the night there.

One of the sailors spoke French. He spoke to the priest about the war in Europe, and told him the Germans had occupied France. The priest cried. According to the priest, the missionaries came to Lifou in 1896, built the small church and named it Lady of Lourdes. That's why the natives were Catholic. The church had very low sidewalls. It was open all around. The floor was golden sand and the benches were made from chipped coconut logs. A small altar was covered with a white cloth.

Towards the evening, men on the beach dug away sand, made a dugout and lined it with banana leaves. Four men carried a net full of fish of all sizes, poured them into the dugout, covered them with leaves and sand and started a fire.

The priest told us the natives were going to prepare a feast for us. They wanted us to enjoy the visit. The children were going to sing. It was getting dark when the men and women gathered around the fire. Children, mostly young girls, sang French songs. The priest and a woman nun directed the choir.

Somehow the men pushed the hot coals to one side and brought out the cooked fish and handed portions to the women and children. I received a large fish on a wooden platter. It was delicious.

Everybody ate fish, bananas, coconuts, some kind of tropical fruit mixture, and the men drank something that made them laugh. The fire died down, and the women took the small children and walked back to the village. We kept watching the teenage girls sing. In the light of the fire, they looked irresistible.

Maybe we watched the girls too much. The priest bid us farewell. He

14. New Caledonia Again

and the woman nun gathered the girls and walked them up to the little church for the night. The men kept drinking, talking loud, and laughing. For us, the feast was over. It took two trips with the dinghy to get all of us back to the yard boat. The captain knew we were not going to spend the night on the island. The girls were gone.

The yard boat slowly moved away from the island into the darkness. I stretched out on an inside wooden bench and heard the beeper start. That wooden bench was so comfortable, when I woke up it was morning and we were entering Nouméa Bay.

"When is my turn coming?" I asked.

It was the beginning of November. About half of the original guys of the company had gone back to the U.S. They were the lucky ones. Every time a departing list was published, my name was not on it.

Soon, I couldn't name most of the men in the mess hall. They seemed so young, probably drafted a few months ago. They appeared restless and they talked loud. I wondered how they would react under fire.

I remembered what the first sergeant said to us, "Teach them all you know." Somehow I felt obligated to do so, and I knew my other buddies felt the same way. I even had some fun trying to teach a few new men how to drive my big bin truck, how to double clutch from gear to gear, going up or going down a hill, or being caught on a beach during an air attack. They listened and wanted to learn.

Hoping to find his name on the next list of men departing for the U.S. was everybody's dream. For me, the dream wasn't there. I complained to the first sergeant that of the original group of men in the small arms department, I was the last man left.

"When is my turn coming?" I asked.

The first sergeant told me I had a high M.O. number (Military Occupation Specialty). They had to get someone with the same number to replace me.

Then he said, "Quit complaining. I think your name is on the next list."

The sergeant was right. My name was on the next list. It was a short list with only four men departing Nouméa, November 25, 1944, on the U.S.S. *Samaritan*, a hospital ship. We had a few days to get ready, to pack our few belongings and say our goodbyes. We were told to be careful with what we tried to take home with us because all bags would be searched before getting off the ship in the U.S., but I had to take that chance. I took the bullets out of my .38 special revolver, stuffed it in a few socks and hid it in my barracks bag. I had carried my trustworthy sidearm on my hip for the last two years. I just couldn't leave my friend behind.

The hospital ship was white with a big red cross painted at its center. We were assigned two men to a cabin, with a shower and a latrine. This was traveling first class. How much better could it be?

My good friend Tommy Mitchell was my cabin shipmate. I liked Tommy. He was from Flint, Michigan, and his family worked at the Buick manufacturing plant. He hoped to get a job there after the war.

The ship was divided into two parts. Everything above the main deck was the hospital section for the sick and wounded. Everything below the main deck was the crew's quarters, the cabins for the soldiers and Marines traveling back to the U.S., and a large mess hall with tables and benches to sit on. In the chow line, the cooks asked the men how they wanted their eggs, or did they want their hamburgers well done. At first I thought they were kidding, but they were not.

On one deck, there was an exercise room, and at night there was a movie played in a small theater. If you got there early enough you got a seat. A couple well organized poker games were started down in the ship's cargo section. I was a pretty good poker player. I thought I'd give it a try someday.

Over the loudspeaker, they revealed the port of entry for the sick and wounded and the Marines would be San Diego, California, December 8, 1944. Port of entry for the army personnel would be Los Angeles, California, December 9, 1944. The ship would travel without escort and there would be no stops.

Each beautiful day was followed by another beautiful day. The water was glass smooth. The ship traveled at high speed and sometimes it zigged and sometimes it zagged.

On deck, the men read books, slept or just relaxed. I spent my time on deck and a few hours a day down in the hole playing poker. I was lucky. I was about $1000 ahead.

At least two poker games were going on at all times. All you had to do was wait for a little while. Someone would drop out of a game and you took his seat. The big winner in the hundred dollar limit game was an Asian crewman. Every time he won a pot he laughed and made fun of the losers. I couldn't understand when he talked, but I knew he was buying most of the pots with his winnings. He was rattling the players to his advantage.

14. New Caledonia Again

From men's sweaty hands, the dollar bills shrank in size and became thicker. The winners, to condense their piles of money, were buying higher notes, six dollars for a five, twelve dollars for a ten, and up to twenty-five dollars for a twenty dollar bill. They stuck the bigger bills under their shirts, against their bodies for safekeeping. It was very hot, the men were sweating and the place didn't smell very good either. When I went down into the hole that evening, the six men playing in the big game moved over and made room for me. The Asian guy was there, everybody talked about how big a winner he was, but for me, he was a big loud mouth jerk. I wished I could cook his goose; draw poker was my game.

The evening dragged on, it was a boring game. I won a few small hands but nothing big. I was ready to quit for the night when it happened. In my next hand I was dealt a pair of aces, somebody opened and everybody called. The men drew their cards.

The Asian drew one card. I drew three cards, an ace and two fives. In my hand I was holding a full house, aces and fives, a very good poker hand. The men bet, called, raised, and counter-raised. Every time it was the Asian's bet he raised it a hundred dollars and I called the bet and raised him back. Some of the men dropped out of the game and then it was only the Asian and me. The pot grew to more than two thousand dollars. The Asian was on his knees, holding his cards against his chest. He wasn't laughing. He had fire in his eyes and he was talking to himself.

He finally raised me. I was going to raise him back. He also knew I had the best hand, but his arrogance didn't let him quit, and he wasn't going to buy this pot. It was his call.

"I see you!" He shouted, "I see you cards! Show me your cards!" I laid down my three aces and two fives. Everybody looked and the Asian threw his cards into the mix and rattled off something like, "You lucky bastard!" Maybe it only sounded that way.

I smiled, gathered the money and walked away from the game. In our cabin, Tommy Mitchell and I counted the money. That pot was $2637.00. Later we found out the Asian was backed by other crewmen. They split the winnings and that's why he was always there. The Asian was pretty good at how he played the game, but wishful betting in a poker game doesn't beat a full house.

15.

I See Land

That morning we were told our ship would enter the port of San Diego within the next few hours. The Marines, the sick and wounded would disembark there first. All army personnel would stay on board to travel and disembark in the port of Los Angeles the next morning.

After a very fast breakfast, Tommy Mitchell and I ran to the forward part of the main deck. It was early. It was a nice morning. It was December 8, 1944. The men were gathering on deck, holding onto the side rails and looking at the horizon. Over the port side of the ship we could see a navy ship going the same way, most likely our escort into port. It was the first ship we had seen since we left New Caledonia.

The Pacific was so beautiful, so big, but there had to be an end someplace. We had to be close. I couldn't tell what came first, the three consecutive loud blasts of the ship's whistle or the guy screaming, "I see land!"

Land appeared forward and on the starboard side of the ship. We were traveling northeast along the U.S. coastline. Men broke out in cheers, waving their arms and some wiping tears from their eyes.

Somebody hollered, "Welcome home, G.I.s!" I wanted to say something smart and memorable to Tommy Mitchell, but I choked up and so did he. I shook his hand.

Before long we watched the ship enter the port and dock at a large pier, where a military band was playing " The Stars and Stripes Forever." The pier was lined with busses, trucks, and ambulances, and a group of men, women and young girls waving flags was a real welcoming committee.

The Marines were first to get off the ship. Some of them knelt and kissed the ground. Others bent over and touched the ground with their hands as they walked and got on the busses.

The women and young girls were passing out little bags of candy or

15. I See Land

cigarettes to the Marines, and the Marines in turn kissed the girls and laughed.

When the Marine-filled busses cleared the pier, the hospitalized men started moving down the ship's exit ramp. Men with bandaged arms, legs and heads walked down the ramp. Some were helped by nurses, some were in wheelchairs, and some were carried on stretchers to the nearby ambulances. Almost all of them, one way or another tried to reach and touch the ground. They really paid the price.

That very moment I realized how much this country meant to me. I loved my country. I fought for it. I was proud to be an American.

"When I get off the boat tomorrow, I too am going to kiss the ground," I thought, "I wonder what my parents are going to say when I call them and tell them I am in the United States in California." I decided I was going to tell them, "I'll be home soon." I thought, "Will my mother cry when she sees me?" I was much thinner and my skin was very dark from the tropical sun. "Will my mother have breaded pork chops and home fries for me when I get home?" That was my favorite dish. "If I had to make a bet, knowing my mother, I would bet that she will."

It was dark when the ship pulled out of the San Diego port. Like most of the men, Tommy and I spent a long time on deck watching the lights on the coastline as the ship sailed north. The next morning the ship entered the port of Los Angeles. The dock was full of busses and a welcoming group of people were waving small flags. When we walked off the ship I kissed the ground, waved to the people and got on the bus. The trip to Camp Ord, about 115 miles north of Los Angeles, took about two hours. In camp we were assigned a bunk, had lunch and were issued new clothes. We were told we could go to Los Angeles, busses would take us there, but we must be back by 6 A.M. the next morning to await orders to board a train going east.

Tommy and I went to Los Angeles, found the nearest post office and mailed the money I won in the poker game home to my father. We asked about and found a highly recommended steak house at a lower level of a fancy hotel. We had a few drinks and enjoyed the steaks.

The streets were filled with people. Some stopped and said, "Hello." A group of young teenage girls stopped and talked to us. One of the girls had a large letter "V" on her blouse.

I said, "V for victory?"

The young girl laughed and said, "V for virgin. You guys were not here!" I thought that was funny.

Bars were crowded with GIs just off the boat just like us. The young ladies there seemed very happy having more than one suitor at their sides. Drink flowed from all directions.

It was past midnight. I was sitting at a bar having another drink. Tommy Mitchell was sitting at a small table close by with his head on his arms on the table — asleep.

I heard someone bouncing car keys on the bar. I looked.

A lady sitting at the next stool next to me pointed her finger at Tommy and said to me, "What are you going to do with your friend? He's drunk."

On board ship we were told to watch out for people who prey on returning soldiers. Most are robbed or cheated out of what little money they may have. I remembered that, but this lady seemed very nice. She was about 35 years old and had a nice looking girlfriend sitting next to her. The lady spoke to me again.

She said, "If you intend to go back to your camp, my friend and I will drive you to the bus location. This will be our Christmas present to you guys. My name is Erica."

I thought she was pretty. She asked me for my name and wanted to know if we had just come back from the war in the Pacific. I told her my name, that we just got off the boat and were glad to be back in the U.S.A. She introduced me to her girlfriend, Barbara, sitting next to her.

She said, "Barb and I live in the same building in adjoining apartments. We've been friends since high school." Barbara was very pretty, well tanned, with blonde hair, and of the two, she would have been my choice. For a moment I thought, "What do I have to lose?" It was late and I didn't even know where to go to get the bus to get back to Camp Ord. "If these girls are willing to help, what's wrong with that?"

I patted Tommy on his shoulder to wake him up. He looked up.

I said, "These beautiful girls are going to drive us to the bus station. We have to get back to camp. Wake up."

Tommy picked up his head, looked around and said, "Where are the beautiful girls?" He sobered up fast. In a little while the two girls, Tommy, and I were sitting at the little table listening to the girls tell us their stories.

Erica told us she came to California from a little town in Montana. She wanted to get into the movies. Barbara Bentree said her name befitted a movie star, but she married a merchant marine who spent all of his time on the oceans and she was very lonely.

15. I See Land

I offered to buy a round of drinks, but the girls were eager to go. We got to the car, got in, but never got to the bus station. Erica had a lovely apartment.

She said, "You guys can spend the night here with us. Barb and I will drive you to Camp Ord in the morning.

It was a very warm and exciting night. Erica was very aggressive, but gentle and entertaining. I'm not sure, I might have slept an hour or so.

Erica and I were having coffee when Tommy and Barbara came into the apartment and joined us. Both of them were smiling.

On our way to Camp Ord, Tommy remembered he left his dog tags hanging on Barb's bedpost. He asked Barb to drop his dog tags in any mailbox.

He said, "The postman will know where to find me."

In camp we thanked the girls for a wonderful night, for the ride to camp, and kissed them goodbye. I knew I'd never see them again. This was nothing more than progress in action.

We found our barracks. A sergeant walking through the barracks kept repeating the same sentence: "The train going east will leave the station this afternoon at 4 P.M. If your name is on the list or on the outside bulletin board, be ready to board a bus outside this building at 2 P.M. Don't miss the bus."

Apparently there was no roll call this morning and nobody missed us. It was almost noon. Men in ones and twos were still staggering into the barracks from towns, and some of them looked like they needed a quick overhaul.

Tommy and I didn't miss the bus and the train's Pullman cars were more than I expected, bunk beds and all, first class all the way. Tommy and I shared the adjoining seats and bunks above and below each other. I had the top bunk. The train ride to Camp Atterbury, Indiana, took three days. To me, traveling through the different states was a lesson in geography. Watching the snow on the hills and prairies, tropical sun and beautiful palm trees disappeared from my mind. It was December. Seeing snow for the first time in three years reminded me of Christmas and home. I was almost sure every man on the train looking out the windows had the same thought.

At Camp Atterbury, the soldiers went through a processing system. They checked our medical records, time spent overseas, battle scars if any, and the destination where you were going to spend your 21 day leave. My destination was Cleveland, Ohio. I was issued a to and from traveling voucher, and I was ready to travel.

Tommy Mitchell was going to Flint, Michigan. He and I tried to say goodbye to each other. He was like a brother to me. He was a good soldier. He was my friend. We gave each other a hug and said our goodbyes.

On my way home I was wondering how I was going to meet my mother and father. Would I hug my mother, kiss her cheeks, her hands, and would she cry? I knew my father was a tough guy, but I'd kiss him too. I knew him as a man's man. They knew I was coming home, but didn't know exactly when. I wanted to keep that as an instant surprise.

It was late afternoon when the bus pulled into the Cleveland bus station. The streets were covered with a layer of white snow. The cab driver told me it was snowing off and on for the last few days.

He said, "You know Christmas will be here in a week. Santa is coming. He needs snow to ride his sled."

I thought Santa and his helpers were making ammunition in their toy factory.

When the cab turned in to our street, and I saw our home, my heart doubled in speed. I paid the driver, jumped out of the cab and ran up the porch. The front door swung open. My mother ran out, wrapped her arms around me, kept kissing my face and wouldn't let go. My father standing next to me kept patting me on my shoulder. My sister, Lillian, was standing there wiping tears from her eyes. Then I heard my mother repeating in a whisper, "I knew you'd come home. I knew you'd come home."

I kissed my mother's cheeks and her hands. I hugged my father and kissed my sister. It took a little while 'til everything settled down and we started to talk. They told me since I called them from Los Angeles, they knew I was on my way home but didn't know exactly when, so they kept looking out the windows, hoping I would be right there and then.

What followed were days of festival. My mother outdid herself with foods she knew I liked. Very soon I found I couldn't eat everything she made or drink everything my father handed me. I helped my father set up the Christmas tree in the large living room. Christmas morning as a family we attended Holy Mass at St. Paul's Shrine, a church I attended weekly before the war. My prayer that morning was a prayer of thanksgiving.

That afternoon, my aunts, uncles and cousins gathered at our home. All of them were glad to see me at home and asked me about the islands

15. I See Land

I was on. They were sure I helped win the war in the Pacific. I told them it was still going on. We talked about cousin Joe who was in Europe in the 82nd Airborne Division, a paratrooper, and his brother Walter in the Marines, a platoon sergeant. Cousin Vic was in the Army Air Force. He wanted to be a fighter pilot, but he had a problem with his eyes to qualify. My aunt Rose, his mother, was glad. She didn't want him to fly.

My mother's very close lady friend's daughter, Roselee, was there. She was maybe 16 or 17 years old, a bit tall, blonde and very pretty. I noticed several times my mother maneuvered Roselee to where I was sitting or standing. Many times my mother mentioned her name in the letters she wrote me. When I left for the army I remembered Roselee as 12 or 13 years old, sitting on the kitchen floor playing with our cat. That's how I saw her now. Some of my buddies who came home a few months before me were now home on Christmas leave. Men from the 22nd Ordnance Co., Frank Gornik, Max Hange, Eddy Drozdz, Bill Christopher, and Joe Bargiel were in town. My father let me use his 1941 Buick sedan to go meet with my buddies at an uptown bar. It was great to sit in a nice, music filled bar, drink beer and talk about the places we were. Joe Bargiel was now stationed at Fort Hayes Army Arsenal in Columbus, Ohio. Joe thought I should try to get there too. I'd like it there, and it wasn't far from home. Then Joe made an announcement.

He said, "Margaret Leerie and I are getting engaged New Year's Eve. Mr. Leerie, Margaret's father, and partners own the Cleveland Yacht Club. That's where the party is going to be. All of you guys are invited to come to the party."

In the islands, I heard Joe talk about his girlfriend Margaret many times. Joe was a talker.

He said, "I expect all you guys at the yacht club New Year's Eve. If you have no way to get there, I'll come and pick you up." I told Joe I wanted to meet his beautiful Margaret and that I'd get to the yacht club if I had to crawl.

I broke my promise. I never got to Joe's engagement party at the yacht club on New Year's Eve. Two days before New Year I was sitting in our living room reading the paper and glancing out the window at the lightly falling snow. I had a slight chill. I asked my mother for a sweater, put it on, but the chill got worse, and soon I was very cold. My father thought it was the big weather change for me from the tropics to Cleveland winter and the Lake Erie winds. My mother made hot tea and honey, but nothing helped. I had the cold shakes.

My mother and father piled blankets on me, but by this time my teeth were chattering but I could still think. I remembered on Guadalcanal some of the first guys that got malaria started out being very cold with chills and then being very hot. Somehow I passed that information on to my father and mother and if this was the case, I needed help. My mother called her doctor who gave her the phone number to Crile Military Hospital.

It was dark and I wasn't cold anymore. I was warm and hot. I heard men talking and I saw a stretcher. My mother was saying something to me but the words were garbled.

When I opened my eyes I was in bed in a very lit up room with a beautiful colored cartwheel spinning on the ceiling. It was blue and red and green and pink, turning like a cartwheel or a carnival ring wheel. A man and a woman were standing next to the bed. I heard the woman say, "What's he talking about a cartwheel turning on the ceiling?"

The man said, "He has malaria. He's delirious." I remember I was very hot, and then the lights went out.

I spent ten days in Crile Army Hospital located in a Cleveland suburb. Lucky for me, my parents reached someone connected to the veterans hospital. This was my first bout with malaria. The doctor asked me when I stopped taking the daily Atabrine tablets. I told him the date I left New Caledonia.

He said, "You'll probably get a few slight attacks again and again, but the attacks will be less active."

When I got out of the hospital I felt perfectly well. My buddies thought I was lucky because I received orders to go to Miami Beach, Florida, for a ten day rehabilitation and consultation period.

When I got off the train in Miami, I was one among about 25 soldiers, privates, sergeants and officers. Our next stop was the Atlantic Hotel right on the beach, with beautiful sand, a swimming pool and all.

We were assigned two men to a room and ate our meals at any restaurant of our choice on Collins Avenue. Each morning we attended a meeting listed on a bulletin board in the hotel's lobby. That evening I ate my supper at the closest restaurant to the hotel. My roommate was not a talker. He showed no rank. He was an older guy and he really snored.

In the morning I took my three minute shower, shaved, got dressed and left the room. The note on the lobby bulletin board read, "Army meeting: 9:30 A.M. in the hotel ballroom."

15. I See Land

Breakfast was served in the hotel coffee shop cafeteria style. Two ladies were serving bacon and eggs and fries and most of the people in the coffee shop were servicemen. The coffee was good. In the ballroom, the tables were set up in lines with all chairs facing the podium in front of the room. There was a paper pad and pencil placed at each chair setting, and a flag on both sides of the speaker's podium.

I chose a chair at one of the back tables and sat down. I noticed that all men coming into the ballroom were by themselves, alone just like me. I kept looking around, but there was nobody there I knew. When the chairs were filled and the doors were closed, my guess was 100 or more soldiers of every rank filled the room.

The doors to the ballroom were opened. A master sergeant walked in and called, "Attention." Everybody in the room stood up. A major, a captain, and a lieutenant walked into the room.

The major walked to the podium, looked at the men standing at attention, gave us his name and said, "Before you men sit down, I want you to turn to the man standing next to you and introduce yourself. You never know, he might be your partner in your next assignment."

The men turned from side to side and did as instructed. The men on both sides of me served in Africa and had something to do with tanks. I told the men I was in ordnance and served in the South Pacific. The major was in full dress, about 40 years old, with ribbons on his chest and three small gold stripes on his lower left sleeve, indicating he served 18 months somewhere in Europe. I can remember how he started his speech.

He lifted both arms toward the men and said, "Gentlemen, I'm going to talk to you men about you. Do you want to hear what I have to say?"

The men perked up and shouted, "Yes, sir."

The major stood at the podium for quite a while as if concentrating on what he was going to say and kept looking at the men, almost staring. When the major started speaking he sounded pretty much like my high school history teacher lecturing us on ancient warriors and their theories on how to win wars, how to divide and conquer. The major told us how Adolf Hitler had a dream to conquer the world, his German Army was the best trained army in the world. It was better than the Roman Army, the real conquerors of the known world at that time because the German Army had better instant communications and could carry out orders instantly with their tanks. It was better than Napoleon's army because the Germans had tanks and bigger cannons and large trucks, and they didn't need horses.

But Napoleon's horses or no horses, Hitler was wrong. Now, his army was shattered on the run and the end was coming soon.

The ballroom was stone quiet.

The major continued about how General Hideki Tojo, prime minister of Japan, had a dream, how he convinced the Japanese military that if Japan's navy destroyed the U.S. Navy at Pearl Harbor, Japan could take control of Asia and the entire South Pacific, including Australia. Tojo was a gambler, but he was going to lose. The Japanese Navy was on the run and their soldiers by the thousands were dying in the islands. The end to Japanese forces in the South Pacific was at hand, and now the major was going to tell us why.

Again, the major lifted his arms towards the men and said, "You men opposed them, Hitler and Tojo, you crushed their dreams, you made it so."

The major was waving his hands like an athletic coach giving his team players a rally lesson. His speech lasted about an hour. He covered the war and previous wars in Europe, how men in power used war to fulfill their weird ambitions, and what part the United States played in opposing them.

If I had to describe his speech in a few words, I'd say it was, "Hurray for the USA opposing the villains, love of our country, and for men who will sacrifice all to keep it free."

When the major finished and walked away from the podium the men gave him a standing ovation. The captain walked up to the podium and told the men the meeting the next morning would be somewhat different. Check the time.

He said, "You are free for the rest of the day. Enjoy the beach, the pool, and the scenery. This meeting is adjourned." The three officers walked out of the ballroom.

Some of the men sat around and talked. The man on one side of me fought in Sicily under General George Patton on their march towards Messina. He thought General Patton was the greatest general in the world. He told me his tank commander was killed by a land mine, but he was inside the tank and wasn't hurt.

I spent the afternoon near the pool, watched the people swim, took off my shoes and socks and walked up the beach about a mile. Walking back, an older couple relaxing on the beach chairs asked me if I cared for a rum and coke. I thanked them and talked to them for awhile, but I

15. I See Land

didn't take the drink. I was told at the hospital that after having malaria, drinking alcohol is not good for you. It would bring it on again.

A few soldiers had their pants rolled up, high wading in the warm ocean water. They looked silly. In the hotel lobby, a lady from some civil service organization was passing out swimming trunks to men that wanted them. I thought, "why not." I went over and the lady handed me a pair of swim trunks, light blue with a small red seam for a trim. I was going to go swimming tomorrow.

Next morning in the hotel's coffee shop, I heard the men talking about the day's two meetings. The 9:30 A.M. meeting would be for all personnel that served in the South Pacific and the 1:30 P.M. meeting for all personnel that served in the European and African theaters. I wondered why.

When I walked into the ballroom I knew this meeting was going to be different. About a dozen small tables set along the walls, stacked with paper folders, with chairs on both sides looked like the place was set up for some sort of interview. I was right. When the meeting started there was an officer sitting at each table. A captain at the podium opened the meeting.

He said, "Good morning. For most of you this will be a very short meeting. When your name is called, go to that table and sit down. You will be asked a few questions, you will receive your next assignment and camp destination and your departure time from here. Any questions?"

A few hands went up very fast. Most of the men's questions were about money. The men were caught traveling at payroll time and didn't get paid. I didn't have a money problem, but I remembered the last time I was paid was back in New Caledonia. The officer assured the men that some sort of arrangement would be made for them to get paid. When my name was called, I walked up to the table and sat down.

The officer gave me his name and in an asking mode said, "You're Sergeant Alex A. Kunevicius?"

I said, "Yes, sir." He opened a paper folder looked at it for a while and said, "You have an excellent service record. You just came back from three years in the South Pacific."

I said, "Yes, sir."

He said, "You just had malaria and spent ten days at Crile Hospital."

I said, "Yes, sir."

He looked at me and said, "You're going to like this. Your new assign-

Alex Kunevicius at Ordnance Base, Camp Perry, Ohio.

15. I See Land

ment for Special Services is at Camp Perry, Ohio, not far from Cleveland, your home."

I asked, "What Special Services?" He looked inside the folder again.

He said, "You speak several foreign languages. There is a question here for you. If you were offered an officer's commission, would you be willing to go to Europe for a one year tour of duty?"

I told the officer I was asked that same question once before while still in the islands. Then I said, "No." Now I would have to think about it.

The officer handed me an envelope, my traveling instructions and said, "They'll probably ask you that question again. Enjoy your stay at Camp Perry."

I called home that day and told my parents that I was going to be stationed at Camp Perry, Ohio, on the upper part of Lake Erie, a short driving distance from home. My parents were happy. My father told me he knew a lady that wanted to sell her 1941 Studebaker Club Coupe for a thousand dollars.

He said, "I'll give her a deposit to hold the car 'til you see it."

I said, "Dad, I like the car already. Give her a deposit. I'll buy the car."

Within a week I was home. I bought the Studebaker Club Coupe from the lady, went downtown, got new plates and a new driver's license. My old driver's license expired almost four years earlier. I loved my new car, two-toned green, stick shift with radio and heater. How much better could it be?

After a few very happy days at home with my parents, I drove my car to Camp Perry, Ohio. At the entrance gate I was directed to the camp's headquarters. I believe I really confused the master sergeant that met me there. I handed him the envelope I was given by the interviewing officer in the Miami Beach Hotel.

The sergeant kept looking at me then inside the envelope and said, "I'm Sergeant Alberts. How did you get here?"

I said, "I drove my own car here."

The sergeant grunted and said, "What Special Services do you do?"

I said, "I fix guns."

The sergeant looked at the small gold stripes on my left sleeve and said, "You were overseas three years. Where were you?"

I said, "The South Pacific, the Solomon Islands."

585 Raids and Counting

The sergeant smiled and said, "You'll fit in here somewhere."

The camp was named after Navy commodore Oliver Hazard Perry, who fought the British in the War of 1812. It was situated on the shores of Lake Erie between the town of Port Clinton and the city of Toledo.

A soldier showed me to a wooden hut, number T 1405 in row 14, with two bunks, a shower and toilet, fenced off with a few boards, barely hidden from view, and an old heater. To me this looked like the tent city in Fort Knox, Kentucky, where I went through my basic training. It was cold. The soldier handed me some sheets and towels and told me the mess hall was at the end of the rows and gave me the times the meals were served. My roommate was a young man from Kentucky. He had been in the army about a year and hadn't been overseas yet. He told me he was a guard. He guarded German prisoners; the job was easy. His tour was two four-hour shifts in 24 hours with every other weekend free to do as he pleased.

Next morning I got up early, took a shower, got dressed, sat down on my bunk and waited to hear a trumpet or a bugle playing. I waited, but there was no music. The young man in the next bunk was sound asleep. Outside it was still dark and the wind from the lake was ice cold. I ran to the mess hall. It was pretty well filled with men either coming off guard or going on guard duty. The men eating breakfast were too busy to talk. I tried to speak to the guy sitting next to me. I asked him if there were any ordnance men in the mess hall that he knew and where was the ordnance depot? He said he didn't know. He was a guard. I looked for the master sergeant I reported to when I arrived, but he wasn't there.

I walked around the camp and saw the fenced-in German prison compound with some high guard towers a few hundred feet apart and prisoners in marked uniforms walking the grounds. I found the Army PX, bought a carton of cigarettes for $1.50 and asked the clerk where on camp was the ordnance section. He told me the firing ranges and all the ordnance activity was along the lake and pointed in that direction.

He said, "Soon you will hear the gunfire at the ranges. Just go in that direction."

When I returned to my hut my roommate told me they were looking for me.

He said, "I think Sergeant Alberts wants to talk to you."

Sergeant Alberts told me the firing ranges at Camp Perry were used by many army units with some of the men who never fired a rifle. They needed help.

15. I See Land

He said, "You know guns. We'll get you a spot at the ordnance depot. You can work from there."

I said, "When do I start?"

He said, "The ranges are used three or four times a week and you'll find the schedules posted at the depot."

Within a week I got to meet most of the ordnance men at the depot. To me the place looked like an artillery warehouse where cannons were repaired and test fired over the lake. In one corner I found a workbench and a good sized parts bin and some tools. Working at the firing range was not new to me. I worked the range at Camp Leonard Wood, Missouri, before we left for the South Pacific.

As time went by, the men in the mess hall seemed friendlier and accepted me in their conversations and laughter. Most of them were 21 year old draftees guarding German prisoners. I heard them talk about the bars in Toledo, some of them very good places to meet girls. Toledo was a nice city on Lake Erie, barely 25 miles away. I thought I'd drive to Toledo the first chance I got and take one of these guys with me. They knew the best places to go to.

I drove to Toledo and met some of those pretty girls. Some of them even bought the drinks. One pretty young lady asked me if I was the marrying kind. I told her for the moment I didn't know what kind I was. She walked away.

A dark haired beauty told me if her father knew she was in a bar drinking with a soldier, he'd come in and cut her throat and mine too. I walked away.

Almost every weekend I drove home, a beautiful 65 mile drive along Lake Erie. My mother made the best Sunday dinners and I enjoyed being with my family and friends. During the months of February, March, and April the weather along the lake was windy, snowy, and cold, not friendly at all. On many such days, the firing ranges were not in operation and there was nothing for me to do at the ordnance depot. At times I went into the German compound with the guards I knew. The glassed in high guard towers were the most boring part of guard duty. According to the men that knew the best four hour shift in the compound was at the German kitchen and mess hall. The meals prepared by the German cooks were very tasty.

Once in the German mess hall, the German cook handed me a potato pancake.

I said, "Ah, kartoffel pfannen kuchen, vielen vielen dank. (Ah, potato pancake, thank you very much.)"

The German cook's eyes widened. He said, "Machen sie sprechen Deutsch? (You speak German?)"

I said, "Ja, ein kleines bisschen. (Yes, a little bit.)"

The German cook said, "Sind sie ein Deutsch? (Are you a German?)"

I smiled but didn't answer him. The Germans always welcomed me to their mess hall.

I remember this day very well. I was in the hut getting dressed. The little radio was on playing music. It was April 12, 1945. Suddenly the music stopped and a man's voice very solemnly said, "The President of the United States, Franklin Delano Roosevelt, died today in Warm Springs, Georgia." There was a silence for a moment and the announcer repeated the same message again and again.

Within the next few weeks activities at the firing range dropped off noticeably, even though the weather turned better. Daily radio news implied the German Army was falling apart, surrendering in places, and the Russian Army was closing in on Berlin.

May 1, 1945, in Europe, the German radio announced that Adolf Hitler was dead. He shot himself.

In camp there was a feeling among the men that the war in Europe would soon come to an end. May 7, 1945, Germany surrendered. Without notice I was transferred to Fort Benjamin Harrison, a camp on the outskirts of the city of Indianapolis, Indiana. Since I was going to use my own transportation to Indiana, I was issued a gasoline voucher and a handful of gasoline rationing stamps.

At the Fort Benjamin Harrison Reception Center I was told I was going to be placed in a special unit working with the public concentrating in public affairs. Here I heard for the first time about some sort of point system for getting an army discharge. If so, I must have had a lot of points.

I was placed in a unit with men that served overseas in Africa, France, and England; most of them had seen the devastation of war. A few men very proudly served in General George Patton's armored division in Morocco fighting the Vichy French. I couldn't compete with their stories. One great warrior told me he was in hell. He drove a tank and fought bearded monsters.

He said, "All you did in the Pacific was fix guns." He was right. The Good Lord knows, I did fix guns.

15. I See Land

One morning the first sergeant told the men to fall out in full dress uniform, war ribbon and all and be ready to pull some very interesting duty in the city of Indianapolis.

He said, "There has been a request by the city's manufacturing association to have some military men visit the factories and mingle with the workers to boost their morale. All you have to do is talk to the people. Do not interfere with their work. You will see. They will talk to you."

Then the sergeant added, "You will work with a partner. You will work in pairs." The guy standing next to me became my partner. His name was Ron Russell. He saw action in Africa, was a talker, and started almost every sentence with "I'll betcha..." We became friends. He was a nice guy.

At our first factory venture we were met by the manager. He first thanked us for coming and then told us they manufactured and packaged batteries for the military and that 90 percent of their employees were women.

He said, "The ladies know you are coming. They need a little bit of something to boost their spirits, and we'll see how all this works out."

We went into the cafeteria. He said, "Grab a cup of coffee. This is a good place to start."

The first group of ladies, ten or fifteen that walked into the cafeteria, looked to be in their 30s or 40s, in work trousers and some with bandanas in their hair. Some lit up cigarettes and just looked at us.

The manager said, "Ladies, I want to introduce to you these two men who just came back from fighting for our freedom, Corporal Ron and Sergeant Alex. Ask them anything you want."

The women because friendly very fast. They offered cigarettes, pop, candy bars. Most of them asked the same questions. Where were you, how long were you there and did you see any Germans or Japs? They were intrigued by the war ribbons, wanted to know what each one meant and why some ribbons had bronze stars in them. Some of them talked about their husbands and boyfriends who were in the service. One lady asked me if the men in battle zones got enough to eat. Her husband was a big eater. I assured her the men have enough to eat. Maybe I exaggerated just a little bit. I didn't want her to worry.

We got to walk through the factory, watched women work at their machines, ate their sandwiches at lunch time and told the ladies some war stories.

585 Raids and Counting

Ron and I enjoyed the day. The factory management must have thought we did them some good. We returned to the same factory the next day.

I thought this unusual duty would end soon but it didn't. Men were assigned to different factories on a daily and sometimes on a weekly basis, and the men started talking. Some ladies made offers of an evening at home, dinner and maybe a movie, or whatever else.

Ron and I stayed partners. At one factory a young lady handed me a silver pocket flask filled with brandy. She said she wanted to thank me for being a good soldier. She was a pretty young lady. I thought she was going to ask me to visit her at her home, but she didn't.

Since Fort Benjamin Harrison was but a few miles from downtown Indianapolis, the men had no reason to spend their evenings in camp. The bars in town were very friendly, and the USO clubs held dances several times a week. My little 1941 Studebaker was a very handy tool. The friendly girls always supplied me with gasoline rationing tickets, and at times the competing price of gasoline was five gallons for a dollar. Not bad for a guy that fixed guns.

What a great time for U.S. history this was. Germany surrendered and the men from Europe were coming home. Japan was holding on for dear life and it would not be long now. In the barracks, men's conversations turned to army discharges, and there always was that guy that knew it all.

"There is a point system, you know. If you have 85 points or more you'll get your discharge and the system is easy to count."

You got 1 point for each month in service.
You got 1 point for each month overseas.
You got 5 points for each Bronze Star.
You got 5 points for a Purple Heart medal.

I counted my points. I had 53 months of service, 35 months overseas, and 4 Bronze Stars for 108 points.

My friend Ron Russell counted his points. He had 89 but he was a gambler.

He said, "You have more points than I have, but I betcha a bottle of good scotch I get my discharge before you do."

I said, "Ron, you're such a nut. Why would you bet against a sure thing?"

He said, "The army wants to keep you in the army. You're not going anywhere." I thought about that for awhile.

I said, "Ron, if you win not only will I buy you a bottle of scotch, I'll drive you anywhere you want to go before I go home."

15. I See Land

He said, "You have a deal!"

Ron lost. I never got the bottle of scotch.

We were approaching the last weekend in July. For us, weekends were free and I had plans. I had met two very pretty sisters and was dating the younger one, and we had plans for that weekend.

That morning I heard my name called. It was like a dream, maybe like listening to birds flying through the air or you hear someone singing but there's nobody there, but I heard my name called.

The sergeant read off the names. He said, "Tomorrow morning you men will be transported to the Separation Center at Camp Atterbury, Indiana. There you will be discharged from the United States Army."

I heard that loud and clear, "You will be discharged from the United States Army."

It was Sunday, July 29, 1945. At the Separation Center at Camp Atterbury, I was sitting at an officer's desk as he was going through my service records. He read off my time served in the army, my time overseas, battle ribbons and Bronze Stars.

He handed me my Army discharge documents then added, "I have a note for you from the war department. They are making you an offer for a job in the U.S. Civil Service as an ordnance instructor at any ordnance post in the country of your choice. Your time served in the army will count towards your retirement and pension."

The officer kept looking at me waiting for an answer, then said, "Young man, if I were you, I would really consider this offer."

I said, "Thank you, sir, I will." I gave the officer a hand salute and walked out of the Separation Center with my discharge in my hands.

The following weekend at an uptown nightclub sitting at the bar a few of my army buddies and I were celebrating our discharges. The place was crowded with military men and women enjoying the evening.

I looked up and saw her.

She was coming my way.

Two Navy Waves followed by two Canadian officers entered the nightclub and were led along the bar to a nearby table. In her light summer uniform, with her hat to one side, showing off her beautiful flowing hair and a light glow around her shoulders. I thought she was ravishing.

As she walked by me I reached for her hand, looked into her eyes and said, "Now that I found you, I'll never let you go."

I don't know where that came from; I had never said anything like

585 Raids and Counting

that before to anyone. Surprised, she pulled back slightly, then smiled at me and for a few seconds let me hold her hand. Her companions stopped, gave me an odd look, walked by and sat down at a nearby table.

My buddies wanted to know, what did I say to that beautiful Wave and why did I grab her hand? I said, "I think I'm in love with her already, and I don' t even know her name. I'm going to go over there and get her." My buddies told me, "Those Canadians will kill you!"

I went over to the table, got her, and walked her out of that nightclub holding her hand. I don't remember, but whatever I told her was a blessing. Her name was Freda. She was stationed in Cleveland doing Navy payrolls. She was discharged from the Navy one and a half years later and we were married. We had three sons, James, Raymond and Richard, seven grandchildren and 3 great-grandchildren.

Not long ago, I heard a lady friend ask Freda, "Just how many years were you guys married?"

I heard Freda answer loud and clear. She said, "64 years and counting."

Index

Aberdeen Proving Ground 118, 120
Africa 183, 185, 191
Airborne 82 Division 181
Alberts, Sgt. 187, 188
Alex 42, 47, 48, 52, 74, 87, 88, 95, 100, 104, 113, 165, 167, 168, 169, 191
Alexander the Great 134
Americal Division 2, 70
Amsterdam 27
Ankeny, John 4, 146, 147
Annabell 148, 149
Aphrodite, Princess 26
April 12, 1945 190
Asia 175, 184
Atabrine 91, 137, 140, 182
Atlantic Hotel 182
Atlantic Ocean 15, 21
Atterbury Camp 179, 193
August 1943 152, 154
Austen, Mount 100, 102, 109, 110, 130, 132, 134
Australia 1, 27, 31, 34, 36, 41, 61, 120, 137, 139, 145, 159, 164, 165, 166, 168, 170, 184

Balboa 21, 22
Balog, John 6
Banyan tree 154
B.A.R. 171
Bargiel, Joe 6, 14, 22, 29, 56, 59, 66, 67, 70, 82, 85, 86, 87, 89, 92, 95, 98, 109, 139, 147, 166, 169, 181
Bauer, Capt. Frank 19
Belgium 165
Bentree, Barbara 178, 179

Berlin 190
Bertie, James 6, 8, 9, 18, 22, 24, 25, 27, 31, 34, 39, 46, 53, 56, 67, 68, 70, 71, 74, 77, 98, 102, 103, 104, 120, 123, 124, 141, 147, 151, 153, 166, 169
Bin truck 146, 147, 153
Bleu Army 4
Bloody Ridge 114
Boessneck, Arthur 6, 7, 67, 70, 71, 139
Bora Bora 25, 26, 27
Bougainville 139, 145, 166
Brazil 18
Bridwell, Sgt. George 4, 17
Bronso, Sgt. Tipper 78, 85, 90, 92
Bronze Star 192
Brooklyn ship docks 1, 14
Brown, Joe E. 108
Buick (1941) 181
Burton, John 67, 166

California 12, 13, 167, 178, 179, 180, 181
Canada 193, 194
Cape Esperance 134, 136
Caribbean Islands 18
Caribbean Sea 21
Carlson, Col. Evans F. 78, 109, 116, 117, 118
Carr, Myra 34, 35, 137
Cathedral, St. Joseph's 40, 56, 58, 60, 69, 168
Catholicism 13, 20, 56, 109, 171, 172
Chiang Kai-Shek 116
Christmas 106, 108, 109, 110, 121
Christopher, Bill 9, 13, 181

Index

Clark, Ralph 5, 39, 46, 47, 56, 67, 68, 85, 86, 87, 88, 98, 100, 121, 132, 151
Cleveland 1, 56, 169, 180, 181, 187, 194
Cleveland Yacht Club 181
Clinton, Port 188
Coconut Grove 78, 89
Collins, Gen. J.L. 150
Collins Ave. 182
Columbus, Ohio 181
Conti, Capt. Paul 145, 148, 155
Cox 67, 97, 135
Coyle, Capt. William 4, 12, 13, 17, 33, 38, 39, 44, 53, 67, 122, 123, 124, 129, 131, 132, 138, 140, 141, 142
Crile Army Hospital 182, 185
Crown 7, 99, 100, 113, 120
Crown Victoria Ballroom 34
Cruz Point 100
Cuba 18, 21

Davy Jones 26
Dawdell 120
Dear John letter 121
Deboni, Sgt. Lawrence 67, 77, 96, 97, 101
December 7, 1941 1, 9
December 8, 1944 174, 176
December 9, 1944 174
Devils Highway 47
Dorsey, Tommy 109
Drozdz, Eddy 56, 59, 139, 148, 181
Druba, Lt. R.E. 45, 65, 68
Dumbeia Valley 43, 65, 68
Dunford, Father Jim 109, 137, 138

England 190
Enterprise, U.S.S. (aircraft carrier) 82
Erica 178, 179
Erick 116, 117, 118
Ermond 45
Eternity, Island of 2
Europe 18, 35, 160, 161, 168, 172, 183, 184, 185, 187
Evans, A.K. 164, 165

Feast of St. Joseph 37
February 1942 1, 32
Fefie 55

Fiji Island 139
First Armor Division 3
Flint, Michigan 173, 177
Fort Benjamin Harrison 190, 192
Fort Hayes Arsenal 181
Fort Knox, Kentucky 1, 3, 68, 188
Fort Leonard Wood, Missouri 1, 5, 6, 10, 13, 14, 24, 37, 68, 189
France 168, 172, 173, 190; army garrison 50; fort 166; legionnaires 39
Freda 194

Garrett, Sid 6, 22, 67, 76, 83, 84, 85, 87, 99, 100, 102, 121, 122, 132, 133, 169
Gatun Lake 21
General Headquarters 125
Germany 18, 46, 160, 172, 188, 189, 190, 191, 192; army 183, 190; prison compound 188
Gilbert Islands Group 117
God 2, 28, 46, 80, 83, 126, 137, 144, 168, 169
Golden Dragon 27
Goliath 164
Goodman, Benny 109, 159
Gornik, Frank 56, 67, 110, 111, 112, 139, 181
Grable, Betty 137
Great Redeemer 2
Greece 130, 134
Green Army 4
Gridwold, Gen. 150
Grody, Edward 67
Guadalcanal 2, 65, 66, 67, 72, 74, 78, 80, 83, 100, 101, 106, 109, 110, 116, 120, 125, 126, 127, 129, 136, 138, 142, 145, 151, 161, 182

H Deck 15, 18
Halsey, Adm. William F. 82
Hange, Max 139, 181
Harrisburg, Pennsylvania 14
Henderson Field 72, 77, 78, 79, 86, 87, 91, 96, 97, 99, 101, 108, 112, 113, 115, 120, 126, 136, 142, 145, 150
Hiei (Japanese battleship) 82, 86
Hiejo (Japanese aircraft carrier) 82

Index

Higgins boats 72, 73, 74
Hirohito, Emperor 110
Hitler, Adolf 18, 183, 184
Holy Mass 13, 56, 60, 109, 137, 168, 180
Horsley, Sgt. Roy 4, 45, 63, 64, 118, 120, 122, 124, 130, 131, 134, 144, 163, 164, 165

Indian Town Gap, Pennsylvania 14
Indiana 179, 190
Indianapolis 190, 191, 192
Iron Bottom Sound 74, 81, 91, 125, 127

Jacobson, Col. Orrin 64, 118, 120, 124, 125, 131
Jamaica 21
Jamok 161, 162
Japan 1, 2, 11, 12, 20, 46, 66, 80, 81, 82, 91, 101, 112, 115, 116, 117, 118, 120, 122, 125, 126, 129, 130, 132, 133, 134, 135, 136, 141, 142, 145, 150, 153, 158, 159, 161, 164, 184, 191
Japanese automatic weapons 120
Japanese Navy 184
Japanese Zeros 76, 103
Jefferson City 9
Jesuit High School 13, 125
Jews 13, 20
Joanna 120
Jungo (Japanese aircraft carrier) 82

Kall, John 59, 60
Kennedy, John 165
Kentucky 188
King Neptune 26
Kingsholm 35
Kirishima (Japanese battleship) 82, 86
Kolambangara 2, 109, 158, 159, 160, 162
Kost, Edward 6, 67, 111, 112
Kula Gulf 159
Kunevicius, Alex 67, 95, 185, 186

Lady of Lourdes 172
Lady of Miraculous Medal 72
Lake Erie 181, 189
Langlas, Leo 50, 52, 54, 55
Latin 160

Laurel and Hardy 138
LCT 158
LCVP 127, 128, 129, 151
Leerie, Margaret 181
Lentz, Forrest 147, 149
Libby Soap Co. 78
Lifou Island 170, 171
Lights Out 8
Lillian Password 79, 180
Lithuania 160
Lombardi, Guy 159
Longtoms 155 mm. 81
Los Angeles, California 174, 176, 177
Louisa 54, 55
Lunga Point 76, 125, 151
Lunga River 100, 102

MacArthur, Gen. Douglas 20
Madden Lake 21
Magellan 26
Makin Island 170
Mao-Tse-Tung 116
March 5, 1941 3
March 12, 1942 2, 36, 38
March 19, 1942 37
Marines 61, 65, 66, 82, 83, 109, 110, 112, 113, 114, 115, 117, 136, 150, 167, 168, 170, 171, 174, 176, 177; 1st Division 72, 155; Headquarters Command 78, 84, 90, 96, 97; 2nd Division 72; 2nd Raiders 78, 109, 116, 117, 118, 124; 5th Regiment 72; 7th Regiment 72
Massina 184
Matanikau River 100, 136
May 1, 1945 190
May 7, 1945 190
McGawen, Merle 67
McGrigan, John 29, 67
Melbourne 1, 31, 33
Methodism 56
Miami Beach Hotel 187
Miguel, Pedro 21
military police 37
Miller, Glenn 109, 159
Miraflores Lakes 21, 22
Mississippi River 10, 11
Mitchell, Tommy 39, 174, 175, 176, 177

197

Index

Montana 178
Mooney, Sgt. Charles 4, 44, 65, 66, 106, 113, 120, 122, 140, 162, 169, 170, 171
Morocco 190
M.O.S. (military occupation specialty) 173

Napoleon 46, 183, 184
Naru 164
New Caledonia 2, 36, 37, 42, 44, 45, 46, 68, 69, 70, 71, 137, 139, 141, 163, 166, 167, 168, 176, 182, 185
New Georgia 2, 139, 145, 148, 150, 151, 152, 155, 158, 159, 160, 162, 163, 164, 166
New Hebrides Island 42, 72
New York 8, 27
New Zealand 27, 46, 159, 166
Night Fighters 104
North Carolina 158
Noumea 2, 37, 38, 39, 42, 44, 46, 47, 48, 53, 56, 59, 60, 61, 63, 65, 68, 69, 70, 71, 118, 166, 167, 168, 170, 173
November 7, 1942 69
November 11, 1942 71
November 12, 1942 75, 127
November 25, 1944 173

Oak, Jim 140
October 1944 168
Ohio 139, 169, 158, 180
Olasama 164
Ord, Camp 177, 178, 179
Ordnance Center, Maryland 118, 120
Ordnance Co. 22nd (MM) 1, 2, 3, 6, 13, 29, 37, 43, 44, 54, 67, 98, 101, 120, 139, 141, 145, 148, 152, 169, 181
Ozark Mountains 9

Pacific Ocean 12, 20, 21, 22, 26, 27, 81, 127, 176, 178, 181, 183, 184, 190
Palace Theater 138
Panama Canal 1, 20, 21, 27
Panama City 22
Patch, Gen. A. 1, 2, 40
Patch, Alexander 122, 124, 130, 132, 134, 136, 138, 148

Patton, Gen. George 1, 3, 184, 190
Pawell, Edgar 67, 110, 111
Pearl Harbor 1, 11, 12, 184
Perry, Oliver Hazard 187
Perry, Camp 186, 187, 188
Philippines 20, 23
Phillipe 62, 63
Pierre 54, 55
Plentigalk 60
Pluth, Elmer 67
Poland 160
Polynesia 170, 171
Protestantism 13, 20
PT boat 109, 164
Pulier, Jean 42, 46, 50, 52, 63, 137, 167
Pullman 179
Purple Heart 192

Rabaul 145
Rabin, Lt. Benjamin 24, 25, 27, 44, 48, 50, 67, 71, 72, 74, 77, 96, 97, 98, 100, 113, 114, 115, 122, 124, 139
raids 585, 166
Rene 52, 70
Richards, Marlin 66
Roman Army 183
Romans 130, 134
Ron 192
Roosevelt, Pres. Franklin D. 1, 11, 110, 117, 190
Roselee 181
Ross, Barney 86
Route 66 Highway 6, 8, 9, 10
Russell, Ron 191, 192
Russia 160
Russian Army 190

St. Louis 6, 9
St. Paul's Shrine 180
Samaritan, U.S.S. (hospital ship) 173
San Diego, California 174, 177
Santa Claus 109, 180
Sassaville Island 2, 150, 155
Savo Island 2, 80, 86, 127
Scasney, Peter 6, 67
Seabees 77, 87, 90, 91, 96, 97, 99, 114, 142, 163, 164

Index

Segi Point 145
Separation Center 193
Sicily 184
Small Arms Section 44
Solomon Island 2, 65, 83, 145, 152, 166, 168, 185, 187
Sousa, John Philip 16
South Dakota, U.S.S. (battleship) 82
South Pacific 184, 185, 189
Spam 137, 171
Springfield, Missouri 8, 9
Springfield 50 cal. Rifle 143
Springfield 1903 Rifle 131, 147
Stawicki, Felix 67
Studebaker 187, 192
Sweet Skin 159

T-1405 186, 188
Talogi Island 2, 74, 125, 126, 127, 129
Task Force 6814P 1, 70
Tasmanian Sea 27
Tassafaronga Point 81, 91, 134
Tenaru Point 113, 136
Tenaru River 100
Tennent, Conrad 67, 76
Tennessee 1
Tesa 45
Thomas, Berry 15, 31
Tojo, Gen. Hideki 184
Tokyo 109
Tokyo Rose 109, 110
Toledo, Ohio 188
Tommy 178, 179
Toronto, Ohio 65
Tripp, Lt. Charles 145, 158, 159, 160, 161

Troski, Ernie 65
Turner, Lana 137
Turulis, John 9, 11

United States 169, 177, 184
United States Army 3, 72, 100, 101, 109, 114, 130, 132, 134, 136, 188, 193; Air Forces 181; PX 188; 25 Infantry Division 114, 130; 35th Infantry Regiment 132; 132 Infantry Regiment 101, 130, 136; 147 Infantry Division 134; 161st Infantry Regiment 136; 164 Infantry Regiment 72, 100, 109
U.S. Civil Service 193
United States Navy 184, 194
United States Navy WAVES 193, 194
U.S.O. 167, 192

VanBargan, Francis 67
VanMeter, Sgt. Russel 4, 12, 14, 17, 24, 31, 39, 67, 140, 141, 145, 149, 151, 162
Vic 181
Vichy 42, 46, 168, 190
Victrola 159

War of 1812 188
Ward, Aaron 142
Warm Springs, Georgia 190
Washington, U.S.S. (battleship) 82
Washington, George 56
White, Sgt. Joseph 4
winnings 175
Witcolm, Lt. Harold 102

Yanks 33

www.ingramcontent.com/pod-product-compliance
Ingram Content Group UK Ltd.
Pitfield, Milton Keynes, MK11 3LW, UK
UKHW042007140426
5217IPUK00015B/1037